WELCOME TO
I Can't Believe I'm Knitting!
Updated Edition

Yes, you CAN knit! In fact, you're holding all the knitting know-how it takes to add this fun creative skill to your life. Just turn the pages to get instant enlightenment from dozens of photographs showing each stitch and technique—you'll soon be casting on, knitting, purling, increasing, and decreasing like a pro. And our instructions are jam-packed with useful information on tools, techniques, and terminology. We've included 13 projects that you can make as your skills quickly develop. Start simple with a dishcloth or a very *now* scarf, and you'll soon find yourself making sweaters or hat-and-mitten sets for everyone in the family. Look for ***hands on*** alerts along the way to keep you pointed in the right direction. You'll also find Frequently Asked Questions (***FAQ***) and a handy **Troubleshooting** guide to keep your project on track. All you have to do is pick up your favorite yarn and a pair of knitting needles (see ***hands on***, below).

You're just hours away from hearing yourself say, *"I can't believe I'm knitting!"*

hands on

You'll need a pair of 10" (25.5 cm) long knitting needles, size 8 (5 mm) and a ball or skein of medium weight yarn. Look for a icon on the yarn label like this. When choosing the yarn, you may be drawn to all the fabulous fuzzy or variegated yarns, but save those for later. You'll find that working with a light or bright color and a smooth yarn will make your stitches easier to see. You'll also need scissors and a tape measure.

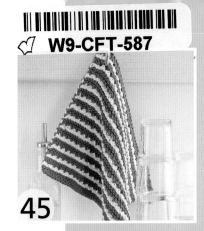

45

47

52

53

58

CASTING ON

Casting on is putting stitches on a knitting needle so you can start knitting. Your very first stitch is a slip knot, so let's start by making one.

MAKING A SLIP KNOT

Pull a 20" (51 cm) length of yarn from the ball. Make a circle at the 20" (51 cm) spot and put the circle on top of the yarn that comes from the ball *(Fig. 1a)*. The yarn that comes from the ball is the **working yarn** and the other end is known as the **tail**.

Fig. 1a

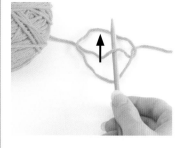

tail

working yarn

Slip the needle under the working yarn that is in the middle of the circle *(Fig. 1b)* and pull on both strands of the yarn to tighten the slip knot *(Fig. 1c)*. The stitch should slide easily up and down your needle because you are going to be working into it later. Don't worry if you pull too tightly—it's adjustable.

Fig. 1b   **Fig. 1c**

Now, let's put more stitches on your needle by using a cast on method called "slingshot." It's also called the long tail cast on. Because both strands of the yarn are used to put stitches on the needle, you need a "long tail."

SLINGSHOT CAST ON

Hold the needle with the slip knot in your right hand with your index finger resting on your first stitch *(Fig. 2a)*.

Fig. 2a

Hold the needle above your left hand and put the working yarn between your middle and index fingers. Spread your thumb out so that the tail end of the yarn is to the outside of your thumb *(Fig. 2b)*.

Fig. 2b

Grab both yarn ends with your other three fingers and hold them in your palm. There will be an upside down "V" of yarn between your thumb and index finger *(Fig. 2c)*. (This is the "slingshot.")

Fig. 2c

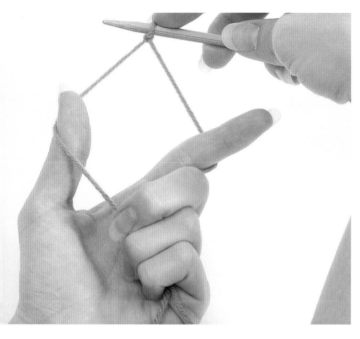

Move the needle down until the strands cross at your thumb. Slide the needle tip under the outside strand of yarn on your thumb *(Fig. 2d)*.

Fig. 2d

Move the needle to the nearest strand on your index finger and slip the tip over the strand and between it and your index finger *(Fig. 2e)*.

Fig. 2e

Bring the needle down through the loop on your thumb and pull the loop on the needle up and out of the thumb loop *(Fig. 2f)*. This loop is your new stitch!

Fig. 2f

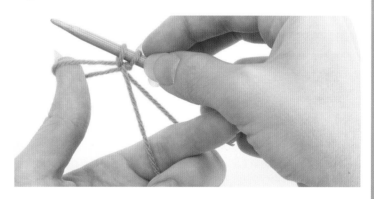

Slip your thumb out of its loop, but don't let go of the yarn ends that you are holding in your palm. Spread your thumb and index finger out again to catch their strands and tighten your new stitch on the needle *(Fig. 2g)*. Go ahead and cast on until you have 12 stitches.

Fig. 2g

I'm left-handed. Where are the leftie instructions?

ANSWER
Knitting is a two handed hobby; handedness is not an issue. The two methods of knitting—English and Continental—differ by which hand holds the working yarn (see below).
Fig. 3a shows the English method of holding the yarn with the right hand. **Fig. 3b** shows the Continental method with the left hand holding the yarn. Many right-handed people knit Continental style just like many lefties use the English method. Both styles produce the same results. Try both to see which one is the most comfortable for you. You will feel all thumbs at first; but, with practice, you won't even have to look at your hands when you pick up your yarn and needles.

Fig. 3a

Fig. 3b

KNIT STITCH: ENGLISH METHOD
(also called "throwing the yarn")

Hold the needle with your cast on stitches in your left hand and pick up the empty needle with your right. Adjust the stitches so that the working yarn is hanging straight down from the first stitch. You may also want to hold the tail loosely with your left hand.

With the working yarn away from you, slide the right needle from left to right into the stitch closest to the tip of the left needle *(Fig. 4a)*.

Fig. 4a

Hold the right needle between your left thumb and middle and index fingers and keep it under the left needle. Wrap the working yarn under the right needle. Then, bring the yarn between both of the needles and over the right needle *(Fig. 4b)*.

Fig. 4b

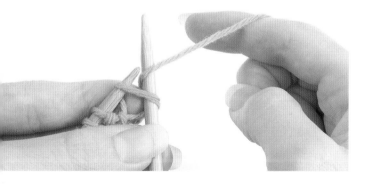

Take the right needle in your right hand. Bring the tip of the right needle out from under the left needle and through the stitch on the left needle,

pulling the loop on the right needle toward you *(Fig. 4c)*.

Fig. 4c

Slip the old stitch off the left needle and tug on the working yarn to tighten the new stitch on the right needle *(Fig. 4d)*.

Fig. 4d

CONGRATULATIONS!
You have just made your first knit stitch!

Now, continue across with the knit stitch. You should end the row with 12 stitches on your right needle.

To start another row, you turn your work, which just means that the needle with all the stitches goes in your left hand and the empty one in your right hand.

hands on
Knit several rows until you get the hang of it.

KNIT STITCH: CONTINENTAL METHOD
(sometimes called "picking the yarn")

Hold the needle with your cast on stitches in your left hand and pick up the empty needle with your right. Adjust the stitches so that the working yarn is hanging straight down from the first stitch.

With the working yarn away from you and held above the left needle with your left index finger, slide the right needle from left to right into the stitch closest to the tip of the left needle *(Fig. 5a)*.

Fig. 5a

With your left index finger, bring the working yarn under the right needle and over the tip from left to right *(Fig. 5b)*.

Fig. 5b

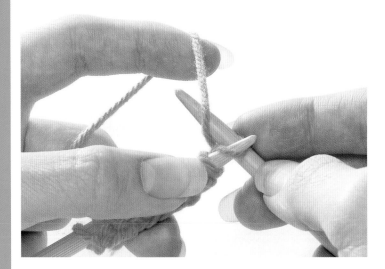

Bring the tip of the right needle out from under the left needle and through the stitch on the left needle, pulling the loop on the right needle toward you *(Fig. 5c)*. Use the right needle to slip the old stitch off the left needle.

Fig. 5c

Tighten the new stitch on the right needle by tugging the working yarn slightly *(Fig. 5d)*.

Fig. 5d

> **CONGRATULATIONS!**
> **You have just made your first knit stitch!**

Now, continue across with the knit stitch. You should end the row with 12 stitches on your right needle.

To start another row, you turn your work, which just means that the needle with all the stitches goes in your left hand and the empty one in your right hand.

hands on
Knit several rows until you get the hang of it.

GARTER STITCH

is name of the stitch pattern you're making, no matter which method you have used. Compare your swatch with the photo below.

Don't put down that swatch—let's learn another stitch—the Purl!

PURL STITCH: ENGLISH METHOD

Start with the needle with the stitches in your left hand and the empty needle in your right. The working yarn should be hanging straight down from the first stitch.

With the working yarn closest to you, slide the right needle from right to left into the first stitch **(Fig. 6a)**.

Fig. 6a

Hold the both needles between your left thumb and middle and index fingers. Going from right to left, wrap the yarn over the right needle and between both of the needles **(Fig. 6b)**.

Fig. 6b

Take the right needle in your right hand. Swing the tip of the right needle out from under the left needle and through the stitch on the left needle, pulling the loop on the right needle away from you **(Fig. 6c)**.

Fig. 6c

Slip the old stitch off the left needle and tug the working yarn slightly to tighten the new stitch on the right needle **(Fig. 6d)**.

Fig. 6d

CONGRATULATIONS!
You have just made your first purl stitch!

hands on
Continue purling across the row; you should still have 12 stitches. Turn your work and purl several rows until you get the hang of it.

PURL STITCH: CONTINENTAL METHOD

Start with the needle with the stitches in your left hand and the empty needle in your right. The working yarn should be hanging straight down from the first stitch.

With the working yarn on the side closest to you and held above the left needle by your left index finger, slide the right needle from right to left into the first stitch **(Fig. 7a)**.

Fig. 7a

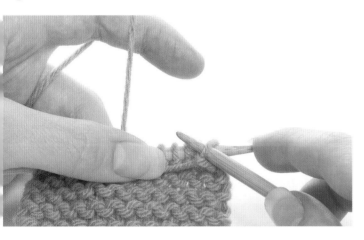

Bring the working yarn around the right needle from right to left and between the needles **(Fig. 7b)**.

Fig. 7b

Swing the tip of the right needle with the loop through the stitch and away from you **(Fig. 7c)**.

Fig. 7c

Slip the old stitch off the left needle and tug the working yarn to tighten the new stitch on the right needle **(Fig. 7d)**.

Fig. 7d

> **CONGRATULATIONS!**
> **You have just made your first purl stitch!**

hands on

Continue purling across the row; you should still have 12 stitches. Turn your work and purl several rows until you get the hang of it.

→ Purl Garter rows

← See the "V's"?

Knit Garter rows →

Right there, where you started to purl, you will see a break in the bumps of the Garter Stitch. On one side, there will be two rows of knit stitches (see the "V's"?) and on the opposite side, two rows of purl stitches.

And, that leads us to—***Stockinette Stitch***!

STOCKINETTE STITCH

is what is commonly thought of as knit: sweaters and hats with a smooth right-side and a bumpy inside.

Stockinette Stitch (smooth side)

Reverse Stockinette Stitch (bumpy side)

And to get this knit fabric, all you do is this—knit one row, purl one row; then repeat these two rows until done.

hands on

Since you ended with a purl row, you should knit the next row, then purl the row after that. Keep alternating a knit row with a purl row for several rows. End your practice of Stockinette Stitch by working a purl row.

Let's take this swatch that you have been working and use it for one more lesson—***binding off***.

BINDING OFF

Binding off is how you remove your stitches from your knitting needles so that they don't unravel once you have reached the end of your project. Since the last row you worked was a purl row, let's bind off your stitches using the knit stitch to keep to the Stockinette Stitch pattern.

Knit the first two stitches.

Use your left needle as a tool to lift the back stitch on the right needle up and over the front stitch **(Fig. 8a)** and completely off the right needle **(Fig. 8b)**. Don't forget to remove the left needle from the stitch.

You now have one stitch on your right needle and you have bound off one stitch. Count the stitch as you bind it off, not when you knit it.

Knit the next stitch; you will have two stitches on your right needle. Bind off as before.

Continue until your left needle is empty and there is only one stitch left on your right needle.

Cut the yarn leaving a long end to hide later. Slip the stitch off the right needle, pull the end through the stitch **(Fig. 8c)** and tighten the stitch.

Fig. 8a

Fig. 8b

Fig. 8c

Binding off in the right way can make a big difference in how your project looks and feels. Unless you are told otherwise, you should bind off following your stitch pattern because the bind off is actually the last row of your piece. In other words, to bind off in purl, you purl the stitches as you bind them off. With a combination pattern using knit and purl in the same row, like ribbing, you purl or knit the stitches as needed as you bind off.

When you are binding off, the most that you will have on your left needle **at any time** should be two stitches. If you have more than two, you have forgotten to bind off and need to "undo," rip back, or "tink" (tink is knit spelled backwards) your extra stitches to get them back onto your left needle (see Troubleshooting, page 12.)

FAQ

How do I "undo" or "tink" a mistake?

ANSWER

Undo or tink is otherwise known as ripping back. The knitting instructors' unofficial motto is "Good knitters are good rippers." It happens to *everyone*. If you have caught your mistake on the row that you are knitting, you can undo the stitches one at a time.

To Undo a Knit or Purl Stitch

Insert the left needle into the stitch below the first stitch on the right needle with the tip of the left needle in front of the left side of the stitch *(Fig. 9)*. Take the right needle out of the stitch above and pull the working yarn to undo the old stitch.

Fig. 9

FAQ

Well, I didn't see my mistake until several rows later. Do I have to undo every stitch on every row all the way down?

ANSWER

You could but there's a quicker way to get there. You will need a circular needle that is several sizes smaller than the size that you have been using. Find the row below the mistake and insert the tip of the needle from the back to the front in the first stitch of the row. Continue across the row inserting the needle in the right loop of each stitch until you have put all the stitches on the circular needle *(Fig. 10)*. Make sure that

you have **all** the stitches and that you have not strayed off the row. Slide the stitches off your needle above and rip out the rows by pulling on the yarn and winding it back onto the ball. Once you reach the circular needle, slide the stitches onto your original needle, starting on the edge opposite the working yarn and being careful not to twist the stitches.

Fig. 10

FAQ

There's a big runner in my knitting! What did I do?

ANSWER

You "dropped" a stitch, in other words, you let a stitch slide off your needle and it naturally ran down. You can pick it back up by using a crochet hook. First, rip back until the dropped stitch is directly below the needles. With the knit side facing you, insert the crochet hook into the loop of the dropped stitch and catch the strand of yarn directly above it with the hook *(Fig. 11a)*.

Fig. 11a

Pull the strand through the loop on your hook. Continue up the "ladder" using all the strands, then slip the loop from hook onto the left hand needle with the right hand side of the loop to the front *(Fig. 11b)*.

Fig. 11b

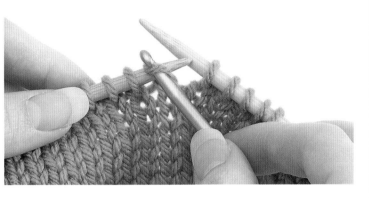

If you are working a pattern that has knit and purl stitches above one another, you will need to pick up the dropped stitch in different way if it made a purl stitch on the right side. On a row that it was a purl stitch, turn your work to the wrong side and pull the strand thru the loop like before *(Fig. 11c)*. This will restore the pattern.

Fig. 11c

FAQ
I was knitting along and wham! I was out of yarn. But when I looked, I really wasn't; I had been knitting with the tail end. What should I do?

ANSWER
This has happened to the best of us at one time or another. There's not a whole lot that you can do, except rip out those stitches or even start over if you have a lot of rows involved. If you keep the tail end wound up and clipped with a paper clip or bobby pin, you will be less likely to knit with it. **BUT**, don't cut it off short to get it out of your way because you need at least 6" to 8" (15-20.5 cm) of yarn to weave into your work so that it won't unravel.

FAQ
My pattern says to cast on 38 stitches. How do I figure out where to put my slip knot so the tail is long enough to cast on all 38 stitches?

ANSWER
If you are using a medium weight yarn, the general rule is that one cast on stitch uses about 1" (2.5 cm) of yarn. So 44" (112 cm) should do it and allow you to have about a 6" (15 cm) end to hide when you finish. Bulkier yarns will use a little more and finer ones, a little less. Four times the finished width of a piece will usually place the slip knot in the right spot, too. If the project has seams, you may want to leave a longer end to use later to sew them and have fewer ends to hide.

FAQ
My pattern said that 12 ounces of yarn was used to complete it. I bought 4 balls of yarn that had 3 ounces in each of them and I ran out of yarn! I didn't lose gauge, so did the pattern list the ounces incorrectly?

ANSWER
Sorry, you got caught in the ounces vs. yards dilemma. Yarns can weigh the same but have different lengths. You need to compare the yards (meters) of the two yarns. If the yarn you chose had 210 yards (192 meters) per ball and the pattern yarn had 250 yards (229 meters), then you were 160 yards (146 meters) short. So if you choose a different brand of yarn from the one in your pattern, you'll have to do a little math to ensure that you will have enough. Add all the yards (meters) of the pattern yarn together and then compare the sum to all the yards (meters) of the yarn you have. If your pattern doesn't list all the information about the yarn, but gives its brand name, you may be able to find out all the information about it on the Internet or by contacting the yarn company.

KNIT NECESSITIES

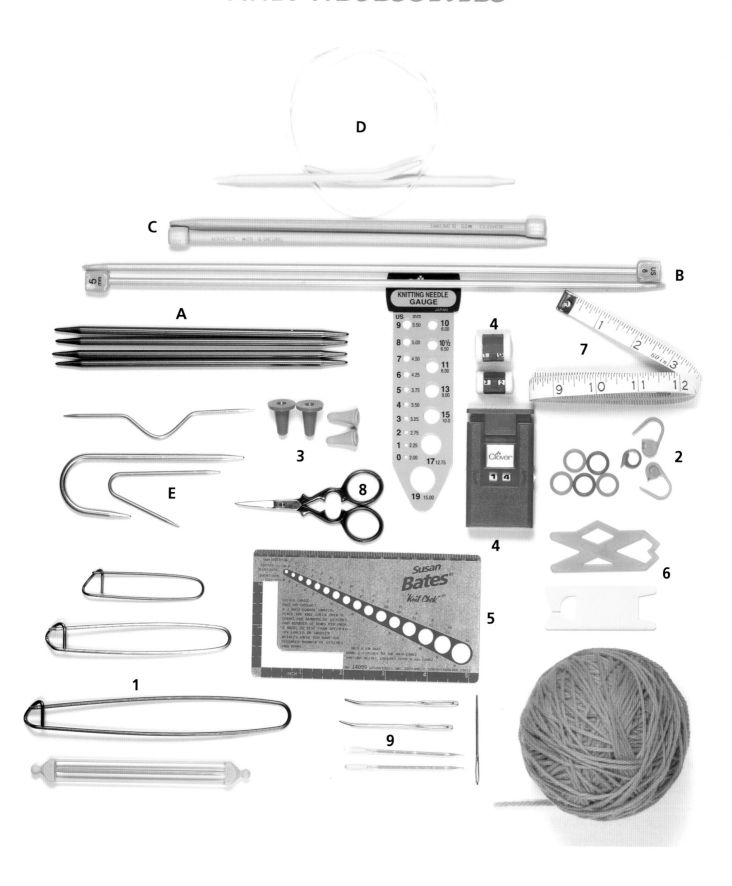

NEEDLES

Knitting needles come in a variety of shapes and materials. No one type of needle is right for every yarn or project and each have merits and drawbacks. Try a variety of needles on your projects. Once you settle on a set of needles for a project, continue to use those, as gauge could change if you switch from plastic to aluminum, for instance. Take a look at a few that are featured on the facing page.

MATERIALS

A. Aluminum needles are very hard to bend or break. They have a smooth finish. Larger sizes can be heavy in your hands.

B. Plastic needles are lightweight and tend to be less slick than aluminum, an asset when knitting with a slippery, soft yarn.

C. Bamboo needles are lightweight, polished, and smooth. They can develop burrs that will catch the yarn, but can be smoothed out with an emery board.

Wood needles are more readily available than in the past and are made from some wonderful materials. They can also develop burrs; again, use an emery board.

SHAPES

A. Double pointed needles come in sets of four to five needles and range from a very short 4" (10 cm) length for knitting gloves and socks up to a 14" (35.5 cm) length.

B. & C. Single point needles can found from a short 9" (23 cm) length up to a 14" (35.5 cm) long. The size is usually printed or engraved somewhere on the needle.

D. Circular needles are a very versatile tool for any knitter. They can be used to knit in the round for skirts and other large round items like the body of sweater. Also, they can be used like straight needles to knit flat items. They range in length from 12" (30.5 cm) to 40" (101.5 cm). You can also find sets of interchangeable needles and cables.

MORE NEEDLES

E. Cable patterns are made by switching the position of the stitches as you work them. The tool that holds the stitches temporarily in the front or back is a cable needle. Cable needles come in different sizes to be used with different weights of yarn. They can be straight, straight with a dip in the center, or curved.

OTHER GOODIES

1. STITCH HOLDERS—They keep small sections of stitches on hold until you are ready to knit them.

2. MARKERS—The round ones fit on your needle and you slip them from the left needle to the right needle as you are working. Markers are placed to indicate the beginning of rounds or changes in the pattern. The split or spring-shaped markers can be attached to an individual stitch or row.

3. POINT PROTECTORS—They are just what they sound like; they protect the points of the needles (and you too, if you should sit on your knitting!). They slip on, keeping the points safe and your knitting from slipping off. Point protectors are available in different sizes and shapes.

4. ROW COUNTERS—If you are knitting a pattern that has a lot of row repeats, these are the goodies for you! One kind can be slipped on a needle. The other is a counter that can be set down on a table or a lap. While they are not automatic, the counters are a big help in keeping track of the rows you have knit.

5. GAUGE RULER—One of the most important tools for a knitter is the gauge ruler. It is placed on your piece so you can count the stitches and the rows to check what gauge you are knitting *(see Gauge, page 18)*. It also has a row of holes that you can insert unmarked needles through to determine their size.

6. BOBBINS—Wind a small amount of yarn on one of these for use in color changes where the yarn is not being carried across the back of the piece.

You'll need a bag to hold all these goodies and all the other necessities of a knitter's life—like a pen and paper, tape measure (7), scissors (8), yarn needles (9), yarn threader, crochet hooks (for picking up dropped stitches, see page 12).

And yarn, of course! *See Yarn, page 17.*

HELPFUL CHARTS

These are charts that can be found in most Leisure Arts knitting leaflets. The Knitting Terminology Chart lists equivalent international and American terms. You may have noticed symbols on yarn wrappers and in the materials paragraph in instructions; the second chart explains those. The last chart lists equivalent needle sizes.

KNIT TERMINOLOGY		
UNITED STATES		**INTERNATIONAL**
gauge	=	tension
bind off	=	cast off
yarn over (YO)	=	yarn forward (yfwd) **or**
		yarn around needle (yrn)

Yarn Weight Symbol & Names	SUPER FINE 1	FINE 2	LIGHT 3	MEDIUM 4	BULKY 5	SUPER BULKY 6
Type of Yarns in Category	Sock, Fingering Baby	Sport, Baby	DK, Light Worsted	Worsted, Afghan, Aran	Chunky, Craft, Rug	Bulky, Roving
Knit Gauge Ranges in Stockinette St to 4" (10 cm)	27-32 sts	23-26 sts	21-24 sts	16-20 sts	12-15 sts	6-11 sts
Advised Needle Size Range	1-3	3-5	5-7	7-9	9-11	11 and larger

KNITTING NEEDLES															
U.S.	0	1	2	3	4	5	6	7	8	9	10	10½	11	13	15	17
U.K.	13	12	11	10	9	8	7	6	5	4	3	2	1	00	000	---
Metric - mm	2	2.25	2.75	3.25	3.5	3.75	4	4.5	5	5.5	6	6.5	8	9	10	12.75

YARN

Yarn is divided into six basic categories. Corresponding icons are found on most yarn labels. Other names that the yarn weight may also be called are listed below.

 - Super Fine; also Sock, Fingering, Baby

 - Fine; also Sport, Baby

 - Light; also DK, Light Medium

 - Medium; also Worsted, Afghan, Aran

 - Bulky; also Chunky, Craft, Rug

 - Super Bulky; also Bulky, Roving

Older patterns may refer to a two- or a four-ply yarn. "Ply" is the number of strands that are twisted together to make a yarn and isn't a real indication of its weight. In the past, four-ply was usually a worsted or Medium weight yarn, but now four-ply can range from Super Fine to Super Bulky. The **only** way to know what yarn to use for a pattern with an unknown weight of yarn is to compare the gauge given on the yarn label to the one in the pattern. Once you have determined the weight, any brand of yarn that is the same weight can be used. You may want to buy a skein to experiment with and knit a gauge swatch to see how the yarn looks in the stitch pattern.

DYE LOTS

Yarn is dyed in large batches called "dye lots." Each dye lot is assigned a number which is printed on the yarn label. Since the color may vary in shade from one dye lot to another, be sure to select enough yarn with one identical number to complete your project. It doesn't hurt to buy an extra skein, just to be on the safe side.

FIBERS

Yarn is spun and sold in a variety of fibers.

Wool is warm, naturally elastic, and holds the shape of any project well. Wool should be hand washed or dry cleaned. 100% wool will felt **(see Felted Purse, page 65 and Felting Basics, page 43)**, unless it is a "superwash" wool, which is processed to prevent felting.

Acrylic is most times less expensive and can be usually machine washed and dried, but check the label first.

Cotton is cool, with very little elasticity. Cotton should be hand washed.

Silk is strong and also has little elasticity. You should dry clean silk.

Many yarns are a blend of fibers, such as a wool/acrylic blend. Check the skein wrapper for proper care instructions.

YARN TIPS
WINDING YARN INTO A BALL

Many yarns come in "pull-skeins," where the yarn is pulled from the center of the skein. In this form, it is easy to keep clean and less likely to tangle or unwind too quickly. Other yarns are sold in hanks that must be wound into balls before they are ready for use. Remove the label and unfold the hank to form a circle. Slip the yarn over the back of a chair and cut the knot that holds the strands together. Gently wrap the yarn around two fingers until a small ball is formed. Remove your fingers and continue to wind the yarn very loosely, rotating to keep the ball uniform. Be careful to wind the ball loosely, for if the yarn is pulled too tightly or stretched while being wound, it will lose some of its elasticity.

REUSING YARN

If you have ripped out a large area of your knitting and want to reuse the yarn, it's a good idea to remove the crinkles that have formed. To do so, wind the yarn around a large box to make a hank. Tie the hank in four places with a different color yarn and remove it from the box. Use a clothes steamer or hold the hank over the steaming spout of a tea kettle for several minutes, taking care not to burn yourself. Shake the hank to allow all the yarn to be exposed to the steam and help remove the crinkling. Lay the hank flat on a towel and allow to dry completely before winding the yarn into a ball.

GAUGE

Gauge is the number of stitches and rows in every inch of your knitting and is used to control the finished size. Most knitting patterns specify the gauge, or tension, that the designer used—and that you **must** match to get the proper size.

Because everyone knits differently—loosely, tightly, or somewhere in between—the finished size can vary even when the knitters use the very same pattern, yarn, and needles.

Before starting a project, it's absolutely necessary for you to knit a swatch in the pattern stitch with the yarn and needles suggested. Since you will want to measure a flat area of the swatch, you will need to cast on a few more stitches than the actual gauge and also work a few more rows. See the example below.

EXAMPLE

A pattern calls for a medium weight yarn and size 9 needles (5.5 mm) to achieve a gauge of 16 sts and 22 rows = 4" (10 cm) in Stockinette Stitch.

Cast on 20 stitches.
Work in Stockinette Stitch for 26 rows and then bind off. Lay your swatch on a hard, smooth, flat surface. Measure to see if you have 20 stitches and 26 rows in a 4" (10 cm) square *(Photo A)*. If your swatch is smaller than 4" (10 cm) square, you are knitting too tightly—try again with larger

size needles. If it is larger than 4" (10 cm), you are knitting too loosely—try again with smaller size needles.

Keep trying until your swatch measures 4" (10 cm) square, then use those needles for your project.

Tip: Write the needle size and yarn type somewhere on your pattern or on a sticky note in case your needles become AWOL from that project.

Photo A

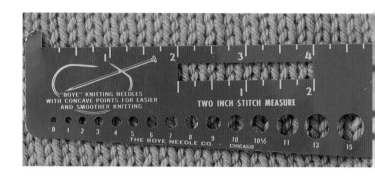

FAQ

I want to start my project now! Why do I need to waste time on a silly gauge swatch?

ANSWER

All knitters are excited by their new projects and there are some projects where gauge doesn't matter a lot—like dishcloths or a scarf. But, if your project is supposed to fit somebody or if you want to be sure to have enough yarn, don't skip the gauge swatch. For instance, if you are knitting a sweater with a finished measurement of 34" (86.5 cm), and your gauge is just a *little* off, say 5½ stitches per inch instead of 5, you may think that's not too bad. However, the finished sweater will measure only 31" (78.5 cm), a difference of 3" (7.5 cm) because of that extra half of a stitch per inch. If you are knitting an afghan, the difference would be even more dramatic.

Making an accurate gauge swatch each time you begin something new takes time. But, you don't want to spend your time working on an item that ends up several sizes too small or too large.

ROW GAUGE

Many times a piece is worked to inches and if your row gauge happens to be not exact, your work will still turn out fine. However, row gauge is very important in some designs, such as raglan sleeve sweaters, where the armhole depth and sleeve cap are determined entirely by rows, or designs where the overall length of the piece is obtained by a specific repeat of intricate stitch pattern rows. If you are knitting one of these designs and you are able to obtain the stitch gauge in your swatch but your row gauge is slightly off, you can correct the row gauge by using a different size needle on alternate rows. Your stitch gauge will not be affected enough to matter.

If you have more rows per inch than specified, use a larger size needle on the wrong side rows; if you have fewer rows per inch than specified, use a smaller size needle on the wrong side rows. Keep trying until you find just the right combination that will give you both the stitch and row gauges.

UNDERSTANDING INSTRUCTIONS

Knitting instructions really look like a foreign language, full of abbreviations, punctuation marks, and other terms and symbols. This method of writing saves time and space and is actually easy to read once you understand the knitting shorthand.

A list of abbreviations is included with each leaflet or pattern, and you should review this list carefully before beginning a project. The abbreviations most often used by Leisure Arts are listed below. Symbols and terms are listed on page 20.

ABBREVIATIONS

BC	Back Cable **or** Back Cross	Rnd(s)	Round(s)
CB	Cable Back	RT	Right Twist
CC	Contrasting Color	sc	single crochet
CF	Cable Front	sp(s)	space(s)
cm	centimeters	SSK	slip 2 stitches as if to knit, knit same 2 stitches together
EOR	every other row	st(s)	stitch(es)
FC	Front Cable or Front Cross	TB	Twist Back
Fig	Figure	tbl	through back loop(s)
K	knit	TF	Twist Front
LT	Left Twist	tog	together
M1	Make One	WYB	
M1P	Make One Purl	**or** WYIB	with yarn in back
MC	Main Color	WYF	
mm	millimeters	**or** WYIF	with yarn in front
P	purl	YO	yarn over
PSSO	pass slipped stitch(es) over		

SYMBOLS AND TERMS

★ — work instructions following ★ (star) as many more times as indicated in addition to the first time.

† to † — work all instructions from first † (dagger) to second † as many times as specified.

AT THE SAME TIME — two different shapings are worked simultaneously, while maintaining the established pattern.

change to larger size needles — replace the right needle with one large size needle and work the stitches from the left needle as instructed; at the end of the row or round, replace the left needle with the other larger size needle.

change to smaller size needles — replace the right needle with one smaller size needle and work the stitches from the left needle as instructed; at the end of the row or round replace the left needle with the other smaller size needle.

front vs. back — the side facing you is the front of your work and the front of your stitches; the back is the side away from you. These terms are used in instructions of increases, decreases, and in other techniques to tell you how and where to put your needles to work the stitches.

loosely — (binding off, adding new, or casting on) the work should be as elastic as the knitting.

marker — a small piece of yarn tied in a circle, a rubber band, or a small plastic ring.

multiple — the number of stitches required to complete one repeat of a pattern.

place marker — slip a marker on the needle to mark or set off a group of stitches or to mark the beginning of a round. Slip it from the left needle to the right needle on every row (or round) until you are instructed to remove it or until it is no longer needed.

right vs. left — the side of the garment as if you were wearing it.

right side vs. wrong side — the right side of your work is the side the public will see.

work even — work without increasing or decreasing in the established pattern.

work across — continue working in the established pattern.

PUNCTUATION

When reading knitting instructions, read from punctuation mark to punctuation mark. Just as in grammar, commas (,) mean to pause and semicolons (;) mean to stop.

colon (:)—the number(s) given after a colon at the end of a row or round denote(s) the number of stitches you should have on your needle.

parentheses ( ) or brackets [ ] — work enclosed instructions **as many** times as specified by the number immediately following **or** work all enclosed instructions in the stitch indicated **or** contains explanatory remarks.

braces { } — work **only** the number within the braces that corresponds to the size you are making.

READING PATTERNS

Let's see how knitting instructions look when written in abbreviated form. Below are two examples of instructions. Under each example, a "translation" of how to read the example is given.

Instructions: Cast on 35 sts **loosely**.

Translation: Make a slip knot, then cast on 34 more stitches, making sure the stitches are loose enough to be worked into.

Instructions: K4, P1, K1, P1, ★ K3, P1, K1, P1; repeat from ★ across to last 4 sts, K4.

Translation: Knit the first four stitches, purl one stitch, knit one stitch, purl one stitch, ★ knit three stitches, purl one stitch, knit one stitch, purl one stitch; repeat each step after the ★ (all the instructions between the ★ and the semi-colon) across the row until only four stitches remain. Knit the last four stitches.

ZEROS

To shorten the length of an complex pattern, zeros are sometimes used so that all sizes can be combined. For example, P2{0-1} means the first size would purl 2 stitches, the second size would do nothing, and last size would purl one stitch.

SLIPPING STITCHES

When the instructions read to slip a stitch, you simply transfer it from one needle to another —usually from the left needle to the right needle, **without** knitting or purling it.
In order to prevent stitches that are twisted **(see Photo P, page 37)**, there are times when you should "slip as if to **knit**," and other times when you should "slip as if to **purl**."

SLIP AS IF TO KNIT

Insert the right needle into the stitch on the left needle as if you were going to **knit** it **(Fig. 12)**, and slip it off the left needle.

Fig. 12

SLIP AS IF TO PURL

Insert the right needle into the stitch on the left needle as if you were going to **purl** it **(Fig. 13a)**, and slip it off the left needle.

Fig. 13a

There are two ways a slipped stitch can be used in a pattern when slipped as if to **purl**.

1. Slip a stitch with the working yarn held on the **wrong** side of the work **(Fig. 13a)**, so that the working yarn will **not** show **(Fig. 13b)**.

Fig. 13b

2. Slip a stitch with the working yarn held on the **right** side of the work, so that the working yarn **will** show **(Fig. 13c)**.

Fig. 13c

Follow this general rule—when you are going to **do** something with the slipped stitch, like use it as one step of a decrease, slip it as if to **knit**; if you are **not** doing something with the slipped stitch, slip it as if to **purl**.

Now that you have learned how to slip a stitch to use it for a decrease, turn the page to learn how to work decreases.

KNIT 2 STITCHES TOGETHER
(abbreviated K2 tog)

Insert the right needle into the **front** of the second, then the first stitch on the left needle as if to **knit** **(Fig. 14)** and knit them together as if they were one stitch. This decrease slants to the right **(Photo B)** and is one of the most frequently used.

Fig. 14

SLIP 1, KNIT 1, PASS SLIPPED STITCH OVER (abbreviated slip 1, K1, PSSO)

Slip one stitch as if to **knit (Fig. 12, page 21)**. Knit the next stitch. With the left needle, bring the slipped stitch over the knit stitch **(Fig. 15)** and off the needle, just as you did when you were binding off. This decrease slants to the left **(Photo C)**.

Fig. 15

Photo B

Photo C

SLIP, SLIP, KNIT (abbreviated SSK)

Slip the first stitch as if to **knit** *(Fig. 16a)*, then slip the next stitch also as if to **knit** (**or**, separately slip the next two stitches as if to **knit**). Insert the **left** needle into the **front** of both slipped stitches *(Fig. 16b)* and knit them together *(Fig. 16c)*. This decrease also slants to the left *(Photo D)* and is interchangeable with slip 1, K1, PSSO. SSK is the mirror image of K2 tog.

Fig. 16c

Fig. 16a

Fig. 16b

Photo D

Decreases are continued on page 24.

PURL 2 STITCHES TOGETHER
(abbreviated P2 tog)

Insert the right needle into the front of the first two stitches on the left needle as if to **purl** *(Fig. 17)* and purl them together as if they were one stitch. This decrease slants to the right on the knit side *(Photo E)* and is the most common purl decrease.

Fig. 17

Photo E

SLIP, SLIP, PURL (abbreviated SSP)

Slip the first stitch as if to **knit** *(Fig. 12, page 21)*, then slip the next stitch as if to **knit**. Place these two stitches back onto the left needle. Insert the right needle into the **back** of both stitches from **back** to **front** *(Fig. 18)* and purl them together as if they were one stitch.

Fig. 18

This decrease slants to the left on the knit side *(Photo F)* and resembles SSK.

Photo F

PURL 2 STITCHES TOGETHER THROUGH THE BACK LOOPS (abbreviated P2 tog tbl)

Insert the right needle from **left** to **right** into the second stitch, then the first stitch on the left needle *(Fig. 19)* and purl them together as if they were one stitch. This decrease also slants to the left on the knit side *(Photo G)*.

Fig. 19

Photo G

When shaping a knit project, you'll probably need to increase, too. The next section shows a variety of knit and purl increases.

BAR INCREASE

The Bar Increase is the most popular and, perhaps, the easiest of increases. It's also known as knitting into the front and the back of a stitch. Knit the next stitch but do **not** slip it off the left needle **(Fig. 20a)**. Instead, knit into the **back** of the **same** stitch **(Fig. 20b)**, then slip it off the left needle. You can see the bar in Photo H.

Fig. 20a

Fig. 20b

Photo H

MAKE ONE (abbreviated M1)

The Make One is used when working increases that will not be hidden in a seam, and is most commonly used when knitting a garment from the neck down. Insert the **left** needle under the horizontal strand between the stitches from the **front (Fig. 21a)**. Then, knit into the **back** of the strand **(Fig. 21b)**. Photo I shows the increase.

Fig. 21a

Fig. 21b

Photo I

Increases are continued on page 26.

INVISIBLE INCREASES

Invisible increases cause some pulling of the knit fabric and should not be used for raglan shaping or when knitting a garment from the neck down.

RIGHT INVISIBLE INCREASE

Insert the right needle from the **front** into the side of the stitch **below** the next stitch on the left needle **(Fig. 22)** and knit it. The nearly invisible increase is shown in **Photo J**.

Fig. 22

Photo J

LEFT INVISIBLE INCREASE

Insert the left needle from the **back** into the side of the stitch 2 rows **below** the stitch on the right needle **(Fig. 23a)**, pull it up and knit it **(Fig. 23b)**. This left slanting increase is shown in **Photo K**.

Fig. 23a

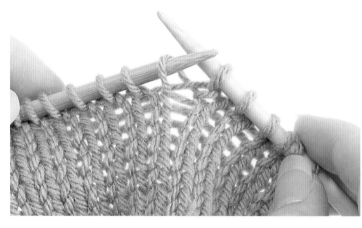

Fig. 23b

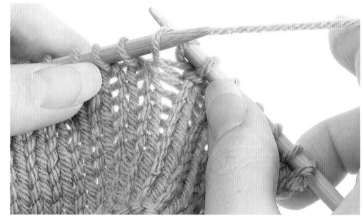

Photo K

BAR INCREASE

Purl the next stitch but do **not** slip it off the left needle. Insert the right needle into the **back** of the **same** stitch from **back** to **front** *(Fig. 24)* and purl it. You can see the bar in **Photo L**.

Fig. 24

Photo L

MAKE ONE PURL (abbreviated M1P)

Insert the left needle under the horizontal strand between the stitches from the **back** *(Fig. 25a)*. Then purl into **front** of the strand *(Fig. 25b)*. **Photo M** shows the increase.

Fig. 25a

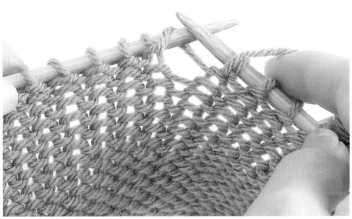

Fig. 25b

Photo M

Increases are continued on page 28.

INVISIBLE INCREASES

Invisible increases cause some pulling of the knit fabric and should not be used for raglan shaping or when knitting a garment from the neck down.

RIGHT INVISIBLE INCREASE

Insert the right needle from the **back** into the top of the stitch **below** the next stitch on the left needle **(Fig. 26)**. Slip it onto the left needle and purl it. This almost invisible increase slants to the right on the knit side **(Photo N)**.

Fig. 26

Photo N

LEFT INVISIBLE INCREASE

Insert the left needle from the **front** into the top of the stitch 2 rows **below** the stitch on the right needle **(Fig. 27)**, pull it up and purl it. This left slanting increase is shown in **Photo O**.

Fig. 27

Photo O

ADDING ON NEW STITCHES

This technique is used when one or more stitches are needed to be added at the beginning of a row or in the middle of a row after having bound off stitches for buttonholes or other openings. It is another method of casting on. If you are adding on stitches in the middle of a row, when you get to the bound off stitches, turn your work around like you are starting a new row. Knit the first stitch on the left needle, but do **not** slip the old stitch off the needle **(Fig. 28a)**.

Fig. 28a

Slip the left needle into the stitch on the right needle from **front** to **back** and slip it onto the left needle **(Fig. 28b)**. Repeat as many times as needed. If you have turned your work to add on stitches to complete an opening in the middle of a row, turn your work around and work across.

Fig. 28b

COMBINATION INCREASES
KNITTING AND PURLING INTO THE SAME STITCH

Knit the next stitch but do **not** slip it off the left needle. Bring the yarn to the **front** (between the needles) and purl into the **front** loop of the **same** stitch **(Fig. 29)**. Slip it off the needle.

Fig. 29

PURLING AND KNITTING INTO THE SAME STITCH

Purl the next stitch but do **not** slip it off the left needle. Bring the yarn to the **back** (between the needles) and knit into the **back** loop of the **same** stitch **(Fig. 30)**. Slip it off the needle.

Fig. 30

Increases are continued on page 30.

YARN OVERS (abbreviated YO)

Yarn overs are another method of increasing stitches. They form a hole in the fabric and are usually paired with a decrease to form lace patterns. Whatever stitch you need to make next after the yarn over determines where your yarn needs to be—in **front** for a purl or in **back** for a knit.

Fig. 31a

1. When a yarn over is **between 2 knit stitches:**

Bring the yarn forward **between** the needles, then back **over** the top of the right needle, so that the yarn is now in position to knit the next stitch **(Fig. 31a)**.

Fig. 31b

2. When a YO is **after a knit stitch and the next stitch is a purl stitch:**

Bring the yarn forward **between** the needles, then back **over** the top of the right needle and forward **between** the needles again, so that the yarn is now in position to purl the next stitch **(Fig. 31b)**.

Fig. 31c

3. When a YO is **between 2 purl stitches:**

Take the yarn **over** the right needle to the back, then forward **under** the needle, so that the yarn is now in position to purl the next stitch **(Fig. 31c)**.

Fig. 31d

4. When a YO is **after a purl stitch and the next stitch is a knit stitch:**

Take the yarn **over** the right needle to the back, so that it is now in position to knit the next stitch **(Fig. 31d)**.

INCREASING OR DECREASING EVENLY ACROSS A ROW

INCREASING

Increasing evenly across a row creates a smooth edge for sewing seams by not increasing in the first or last stitch on a row. To do this, add one to the number of increases required and divide that number into the number of stitches on the needle. The result is the number of stitches to be worked **between** each increase. (If it's not a whole number, round down.)

Sometimes you will need to work fewer stitches between the increases to arrive at the correct total number of stitches. Remember, the point is to reach that total with the increases spaced out as evenly as possible.

EXAMPLE

54 stitches to be increased by 6 evenly = total 60

$6+1 = 7$ $54 \div 7 = 7$ (**rounded down**)

Work 7 stitches between increases (space stitches)

$7 \times 7 =$ 49 space stitches
$6 \times 2 =$ +12 increases
         61 **total**

Since 60 is the goal, eliminate the one extra space stitch in the center, like this:

7 • 7 • 7 • 6 • 7 • 7 • 7

(60 stitches total)

• = stitch to be increased = 2 stitches

DECREASING

Decreasing evenly across a row creates a smooth edge for sewing seams by not decreasing in the first or last stitch on a row. To do this, add one to the number of decreases required and divide that number into the number of stitches on the needle. (If it's not a whole number, round up). Subtract 2 from the result and the new number is the number of stitches to be worked **between** each decrease.

Sometimes you will need to work fewer stitches between the decreases to arrive at the correct total number of stitches. Remember, the point is to reach that total with the decreases spaced out as evenly as possible.

EXAMPLE

60 stitches to be decreased by 6 evenly = total 54

$6+1 = 7$ $60 \div 7 = 9$ (**rounded up**)

$9 - 2 = 7$ Work 7 stitches between decreases
                     (space stitches)

$7 \times 7 = 49$ space stitches
      + 6 decrease stitches
        55 **total**

Since 54 is the goal, eliminate the one extra space stitch in the center, like this:

7 • 7 • 7 • 6 • 7 • 7 • 7

(54 stitches total)

• = decrease stitch = 1 stitch

KNITWISE

When instructed to pick up stitches, use one of the needles and the yarn that you are going to continue working with. Insert your knitting needle from the **front** to the **back** under two strands at the edge of the worked piece *(Figs. 32a & b)*. Wrap the yarn around the needle as if to **knit**, then bring the needle with the yarn back through the stitch to the right side *(Fig. 32c)*, resulting in a stitch on the needle.

Repeat this along the edge.

Fig. 32a (along the cast on or bind off edge)

Fig. 32b (along the side edge)

Fig. 32c

PURLWISE

Occasionally you will need to pick up stitches purlwise or as if to **purl**. You will insert the needle from the **back** to the **front** under two strands at the edge of the worked piece *(Fig. 33)*. Wrap the yarn around the needle as if to **purl**, then bring the needle with the yarn back through the stitch to the right side, resulting in a stitch on the needle.

Repeat this along the edge.

Fig. 33

Picking up stitches leaves a small ridge on the opposite side of your fabric. If you pick up stitches with the right side facing you, the ridge will be on the wrong side. If you are making a collar that will be turned down, it will lay more neatly if you pick up the stitches with the wrong side facing you.

If you have a large number of stitches to pick up, try marking the edge with pins, dividing it into quarters. You can then pick up a quarter of the total stitches in each section. This will help keep your stitches even and well spaced.

If the instructions read to pick up stitches evenly spaced across, try this:

Pick up one stitch in each stitch along a horizontal or bound off edge and pick up three stitches in every four rows along a vertical edge.

It can be easier to pick up stitches using a crochet hook, sliding each stitch onto your knitting needle.

SEAMS

A tapestry or a yarn needle is best for seams because the blunt point will not split the yarn. Use the yarn from which the garment was made to sew the seams. One exception—if the yarn is textured or bulky, sew the seam with a finer, smoother yarn of the same color. Tapestry yarn or an acrylic needlepoint yarn works well. Be sure that the care of the garment and seaming yarn is the same—if the yarn used to knit the garment is machine washable then the seaming yarn must also be machine washable.

SHOULDER SEAMS

WEAVING

Shoulder seams that are joined by weaving appear seamless. With the **right** side of both pieces facing you and the bound off edges even, bring the needle from behind the work and through the center of the first stitch, leaving a long end to be woven in later. ★ Bring the needle over the top of the edges and pick up both loops of the corresponding stitch on the second piece **(Fig. 34a)**.

Fig. 34a

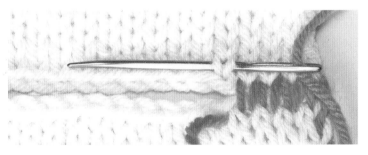

Bring the needle back over the edges and pick up the inverted "V" of the next stitch **(Fig. 34b)**. Repeat from ★ across, smoothing the "steps" of the bind off as you go. Pull the yarn gently every 2 or 3 stitches, being careful to maintain an even tension.

Fig. 34b

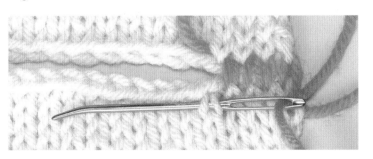

BACKSTITCH

Backstitching provides a firm shoulder seam. The seam should be sewn one row in from the bound off edges. If the garment has shoulder shaping, the seam should slant slightly from the neck to the shoulder, following the slant of the bound off stitches. The "steps" of the bind off may be used like the notches in sewing patterns to help line up the stitches. With the **right** sides together and edges even, weave the end of the yarn through 5 or 6 of the bound off stitches to secure it. Insert the needle from **front** to **back** at the edge of the seam, then bring it up from **back** to **front** a half stitch forward (at 1) **(Fig. 35a)**. Insert the needle back where the first stitch began (at 2) and bring it up a whole stitch forward (at 3). ★ Insert the needle a half stitch back from the yarn (at 1) and up again a whole stitch forward (at 4) **(Fig. 35b)**. Repeat from ★ across. With each stitch, you are going back a half stitch and then forward a whole stitch. At the end of the seam, weave your yarn back into the seam for 5 or 6 stitches and cut the yarn close to the work.

Fig. 35a

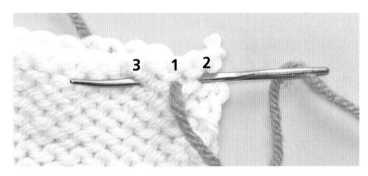

Fig. 35b

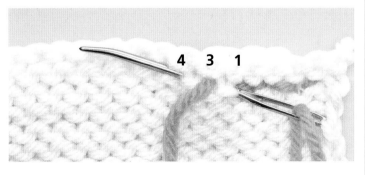

Seams are continued on page 26.

SLEEVE SEAMS
SLEEVES WITH CAPS
The shaping at the top of a sleeve that matches an armhole is called the Sleeve Cap.

Fold the Sleeve in half lengthwise to find the center of the Cap. With **right** sides together, pin the center of the Cap to the shoulder seam **(Fig. 36)**. Pin the underarm bound off stitches of the Body to those of the Sleeve (marked at x's). Pin the Sleeve in place, easing in any fullness. Backstitch this seam one stitch in from the edge **(Figs. 35a & b, page 33)**, with the Body side toward you so that you can follow a line of purl stitches.

Fig. 36

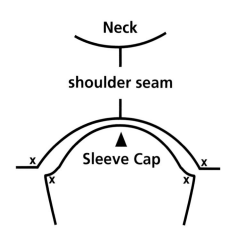

DROP SHOULDER SEAMS
Garments without armhole shaping have "dropped shoulders." Fold the Sleeve in half lengthwise to find the center of the bound off edge. With **right** sides together, pin the center of the edge to the shoulder seam **(Fig. 37)**. The instructions or schematic diagrams will tell you the length of the armhole. Measure this length down from the shoulder seam in Front and pin one end of the Sleeve; repeat for the Back. Pin the rest of the Sleeve in place, easing

Fig. 37

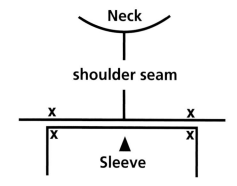

in any fullness. Backstitch this seam **(Figs. 35a & b, page 33)**, one stitch in from the edge, with the Body side toward you so that you can follow a line of purl stitches.

SIDE SEAMS
It is usually best to weave the side and underarm seams because weaving is practically invisible.

WEAVING — ONE STITCH IN
With the **right** side of both pieces facing you and edges even, sew through both sides once to secure the beginning of the seam. Pull the first and second stitches on the Front edge slightly apart. Notice the bars or harizontal strands between the stitches. Insert the needle under the bar between the first and second stitches on the first row and pull the yarn through **(Fig. 38)**. Insert the needle under the next bar on the second side. Repeat, going from Front to Back, being careful to match rows. Repeat this process about six times on each side; pull your sewing yarn tightly and then stretch the seam gently. This helps to keep the seam as elastic as the knitting. Continue in this manner to the end of the seam, then weave in both yarn ends.

Fig. 38

WHIPSTITCH
Whipstitch is not recommended for sewing seams. However, it is great for hems and attaching collars because it's firm and doesn't have the bulk of backstitch.

With **wrong** sides together, insert the needle from **right** to **left** through one strand on each piece *(Fig. 39)*. Bring the needle around and insert it from **right** to **left** through the next strand on both pieces. Continue in this manner, keeping the sewing yarn fairly loose.

Fig. 39

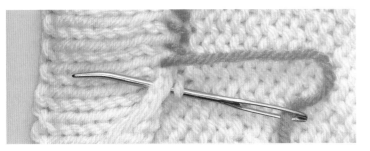

GRAFTING

Grafting, or Kitchener Stitch, is a way of joining two sections together horizontally, without a seam. The stitches are woven directly from the needles. Both edges must have the same number of stitches.

Either hold both needles in the left hand with **wrong** sides together *(Fig. 40a)*, or lay both pieces on a table with **right** sides facing you *(Fig. 40b)*.

Fig. 40a

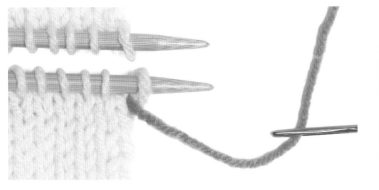

Fig. 40b

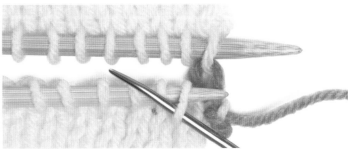

Cut the yarn on the front piece, leaving a long end, and thread a needle with this end. Work in the following sequence, pulling the yarn through as if to **knit** or as if to **purl** with even tension, and keeping yarn under points of needles to avoid tangling.

Step 1: Purl first stitch on **front** needle, leave the stitch **on** the needle *(Fig. 40b)*.
Step 2: Knit first stitch on **back** needle, leave the stitch **on** the needle *(Fig. 40c)*.

Fig. 40c

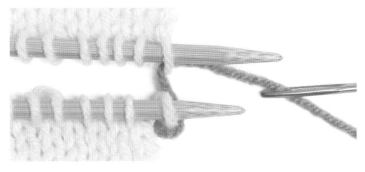

Step 3: Knit first stitch on **front** needle, slip the stitch **off** the needle *(Fig. 40d)*.

Fig. 40d

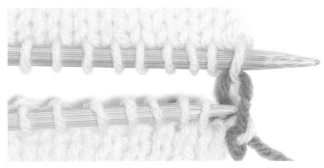

Step 4: Purl next stitch on **front** needle, leave the stitch **on** the needle *(Fig. 40e)*.

Fig. 40e

Grafting is continued on page 36.

35

Step 5: Purl first stitch on **back** needle, slip the stitch **off** the needle **(Fig. 40f)**.

Fig. 40f

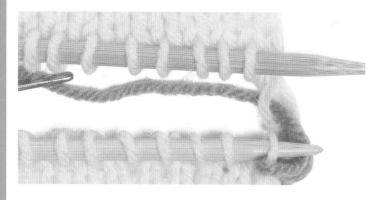

Step 6: Knit next stitch on **back** needle, leave the stitch **on** the needle **(Fig. 40g)**.

Fig. 40g

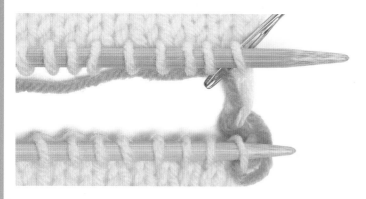

Repeat Steps 3-6 across until all stitches have been worked off the needles **(Fig. 40h)**.

Fig. 40h

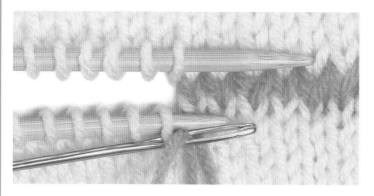

JOINING NEW YARN

The best way to join yarn is to always join at the beginning of a row—not in the middle of a row. The joining will then end up in a seam and will not be visible on the finished garment. If you have four times the width of the piece you are knitting, you have enough yarn to work another row. Finish one row and cut that yarn leaving a 6" (15 cm) end. Begin the next row with the new ball of yarn, leaving a 6" (15 cm) end to weave in later. If you leave the yarn ends long enough, the stitches will not come undone and you do not need to tie a knot. However, if you wish, you may tie a temporary single knot, that will later be untied and woven into the seam.

Sometimes your rows don't have a beginning or an end—as when you are knitting a tube for a skirt, sock, mitten, or hat. When this happens, leave a 6" (15 cm) end of the old yarn and begin knitting with the new ball of yarn. Again, you may tie a temporary single knot.

Sometimes there will be a knot in your ball of yarn. If left in, the knot could work its way to the right side of your piece and you wouldn't want that! So, cut the knot out before knitting it in, then join the yarn back like a new ball.

WEAVING IN YARN ENDS

You have finished your project, so now what to do with all the ends? You have the cast on end, the bind off end, and if you used more than one ball of yarn, you have those ends, too. If you started each new ball at the beginning of a row and left all your yarn ends long enough, hiding the ends on the **wrong** side should be fairly easy. Thread a yarn needle with one yarn end and weave it through several stitches in the seam on a garment or along the edge of a afghan or scarf. Reverse direction and weave it back through several stitches to be doubly sure. Clip the yarn close to the work.

If you did join a new ball in mid-row, untie the temporary knot, give the ends a twist around each other, and weave them in, either diagonally or horizontally. Be sure the weaving doesn't show from the right side.

BLOCKING

Blocking helps to smooth your work and give it a professional appearance. You may block your work while it is in separate pieces for easier assembly, but don't rely on blocking to change their size if you haven't gotten gauge. Check the yarn label for any special instructions about blocking. Many acrylics and some blends can be damaged during blocking.

With acrylics that can be blocked, you simply pin your garment to the correct size (with rust-proof pins) and cover it with dampened bath towels. When the towels are dry, the garment is blocked.

If the garment is hand washable, carefully launder it using a mild soap or detergent. Rinse it without wringing or twisting. Remove any excess moisture by rolling it in a succession of dry towels. You can put it in the final spin cycle of your washer, without water. Lay the garment on a large towel on a flat surface out of direct sunlight. Using a tape measure, gently smooth and pat it to the desired size and shape. When it is completely dry, it is blocked. Another method of blocking, that is especially good for wool, requires a steam iron or a hand-held steamer. Turn the garment **wrong** side out and pin it to the correct size. Hold the steam iron or steamer just above the garment and steam it thoroughly. Never let the weight of the iron touch your garment because it will flatten the stitches. Never steam ribbings, cables, or intricate raised patterns. Leave the garment pinned until it is completely dry.

BACK LOOP

Occasionally you may be instructed to knit or purl into the **back** loop of a stitch **(Fig. 41)**. The result will be twisted stitches **(Photo P)**.

CABLES

There are many variations of cable patterns, but all are based on switching the position of stitches on your needle. Cables can twist to the right or to the left.

To try a left-twisting cable or Front Cable:
Cast on 18 sts **loosely**.

Row 1: K4, P2, K6, P2, K4.
Row 2: P4, K2, P6, K2, P4.
Row 3: K4, P2, slip the next 3 sts onto a cable needle as if to **purl** and hold them in **front** of your work **(Fig. 42a)**. Knit the next 3 sts on the **left** needle. Now, knit the 3 sts from the **cable** needle onto your right needle, being sure that the first st you knit is the first one you slipped onto the cable needle, P2, K4.
Row 4: P4, K2, P6, K2, P4.
Row 5: K4, P2, K6, P2, K4.
Row 6: P4, K2, P6, K2, P4.

Fig. 42a

Repeat Rows 3-6 twice. Notice the cable twisting to the left.

To work a right-twisting cable or Back Cable, repeat the instructions, but hold the cable needle with the slipped stitches **behind** your work **(Fig. 42b)**.

Fig. 41

back loop

front loop

Photo P

Fig. 42b

CHANGING COLORS

When changing colors, always pick up the new color yarn from **beneath** the dropped yarn and keep the color which has just been worked to the left **(Fig. 43)**. This will avoid holes in the finished piece. Take extra care to keep your tension even.

Fig. 43

CHANGING COLOR IN RIBBING

When working a striped ribbing, little "nubs" of color appear on the right side **(Photo Q)**.

Photo Q   **with nubs**

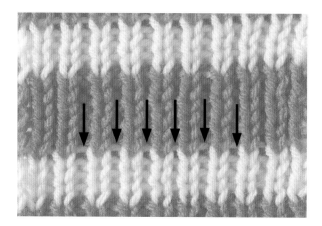

To eliminate those "nubs," knit across the first row of each color change and then continue in ribbing as before **(Photo R)**.

Photo R   **without nubs**

Note: Ribbings have been stretched to show detail.

Like lots of rules, there are exceptions:
1. This technique only works when each stripe consists of an even number of rows.
Photos Q and R show a 6 row and a 4 row stripe sequence in ribbing.

2. When changing colors and working stripes with an odd number of rows (Example - 3, 5, 7, etc.), you would **purl** across when working a **wrong** side row and **knit** across when working a **right** side row.

3. Or, you may enjoy the look of the nubs as shown in the **Socks** on page 62.

CHANGING COLOR IN GARTER STITCH

Most patterns that use color changes in garter stitch will tell you on which row (a right side row or a wrong side row) to change colors. But, if you are stepping out on your own, change colors on a **right side** row unless you want those little "nubs" of color to show.

GARMENTS
SIZING

Most garment patterns are written for at least three different sizes. The instructions usually include both the actual bust/chest measurement and the finished measurement of the garment.

HOW TO MEASURE AND CHOOSING WHICH SIZE TO KNIT

First consider whether you want a loose-fitting or a snug-fitting garment when deciding on a size. Measure around the fullest part of the bust/chest and compare this measurement to the sizes given. Be sure to take an accurate measurement. Choose the size based on the actual measurement or on the finished measurement.

You may want to measure a favorite sweater with similar styling, then knit the size that has the nearest finished measurement.

Once you have decided which size to knit, you may need to adjust the body length and sleeve length in the instructions to fit your actual measurements. To measure body length, place the tape measure approximately 1³/₄" (4.5 cm) down from your underarm and let it hang straight with your arm at your side. Again, you may want to measure a favorite sweater.

When the instructions tell you how many inches to knit before beginning the armhole shaping, you can now adjust this length to your measurement by knitting fewer inches to shorten the sweater or more inches to make it longer.

Measure the sleeve length in the same way you measured the body length, keeping your arm straight at your side.

The only accurate way to determine which size to knit for a child is to measure the child. Measure the child's chest approximately 2" (5 cm) below the underarm and choose the size that has the nearest actual measurement. It is also important to measure the arm length and the body length to make any necessary adjustments to the instructions.

MEASURING YOUR KNITTING

Many instructions include schematic diagrams (below) of the garment. These diagrams indicate the finished measurements of each piece for your reference as you measure your knitting. Always measure your knitting on a hard, smooth, flat surface, without scrunching or stretching the piece.

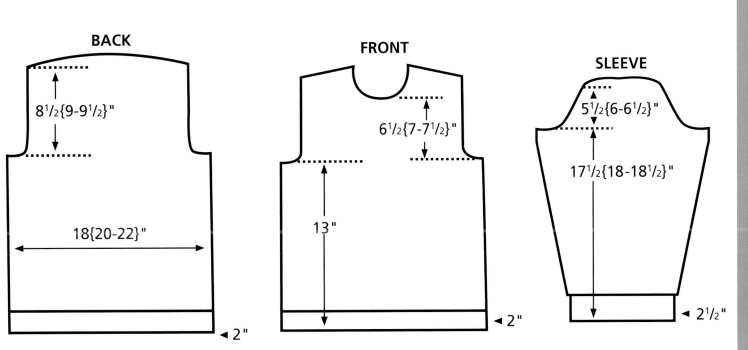

BACK — 8¹/₂{9-9¹/₂}" — 18{20-22}" — ◄ 2"

FRONT — 6¹/₂{7-7¹/₂}" — 13" — ◄ 2"

SLEEVE — 5¹/₂{6-6¹/₂}" — 17¹/₂{18-18¹/₂}" — ◄ 2¹/₂"

Measuring Your Knitting is continued on page 40.

Also, measure the width of your piece every three or four inches to make sure your stitch gauge remains consistent. The dotted lines on the schematics indicate the beginning of any shaping.

Measure the body length to the underarm along the line indicated, from the bottom of the cast on edge to the beginning of the armhole shaping, and measure the armholes from the dotted line to the dotted line at the neck shaping. The sleeve length is measured from the bottom of the cast on edge to the beginning of the sleeve cap and the sleeve cap is measured from dotted line to dotted line.

When measuring a raglan armhole, measure along the line indicated *(Fig. 44)*.

Fig. 44

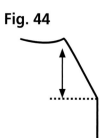

WORKING BOTH SIDES OF NECK AT THE SAME TIME

Not all patterns give instructions for working both sides of the neck at the same time. When instructions are written for the right side of the piece, then, "work left side same as right side, reversing all shaping;" it will be easier for you to work both sides at the same time. This way, you will know exactly when to decrease and all your rows will match.

When instructions are written for both sides to be worked at the same time, the semicolon (;) is the signal for you to drop your first yarn ball and begin working with the second yarn ball.

EXAMPLE
Neck Shaping
Note: Both sides of Neck are worked at the same time, using separate yarn for each side.

Row 1: Work across 25 sts, slip 15 sts onto st holder; with second yarn, work across: 25 sts **each** side.

Row 2: Work across; work across.

Row 3 (Decrease row)**:** Work across to within 2 sts of neck edge, decrease; decrease, work across: 24 sts **each** side.

IMPORTANT: Try to lay your work down with both sides on one needle. Otherwise, it may be difficult to determine which side you worked last.

TIP: As well as knitting both sides of the neck, you may want to knit both sleeves at the same time. Even though both sleeves will be on the same set of needles, each one will have its own ball of yarn. This method can also be used for both front sides of a cardigan. Many knitters prefer this method because it guarantees that both pieces will be the same length.

CIRCULAR KNITTING

When you knit a tube, as for a skirt, hat, sock, or mitten, you are going to work around and around on the outside of the circle, with the **right** side of the knitting facing you.

If your piece is worked in Stockinette Stitch, you have eliminated having to work any purl rows, and you will knit every round. If your piece is worked in Garter Stitch, you will alternate one knit round with one purl round.

Larger diameter pieces can be worked on a circular needle while smaller ones require the use of a set of double-pointed needles.

CIRCULAR NEEDLE

Cast on all the stitches.

Now, inspect the cast on row to be sure that the cast on ridge lays to the inside of the needle at all times and hasn't rolled around the needle *(Fig. 45)*. If the cast on ridges have rolled around the needle, then straighten it out immediately.

Hold the needle so that the ball of yarn is attached to the stitch closest to the right hand point. Place a marker on the right hand point to mark the beginning of the round, then knit the stitches on the left hand point.

Continue knitting around and around **without turning the work**. For the first few rounds, check the cast on edge. If it has twisted around the needle, it is impossible to untwist it. The only way to fix this is to rip it out and cast on again.

DOUBLE POINTED NEEDLES
Cast all of the stitches onto one needle. Then slip a third of them onto a second needle and a third of them onto a third needle *(Fig. 46a)*.

Fig. 45

Fig. 46a

Form a triangle of the three needles with the working yarn attached to the stitch closest to the tip of the needle at the top right of the triangle. All cast on ridges should lay to the inside of the triangle. Straighten any twists of the cast on ridge.

With the fourth needle, knit across the stitches on the first needle *(Fig. 46b)*. After you have knit all the stitches off the first needle onto the fourth needle, you will now have an empty needle with which to knit the stitches from the next needle. Work the first stitch of each needle firmly to prevent gaps.

Knit around and around, checking occasionally, for at least the first few rounds, to be sure that your cast on edge has not twisted around any of the needles.

If you have a set of five needles, divide the stitches between four of the needles, form a square with them, and knit as above.

Fig. 46b

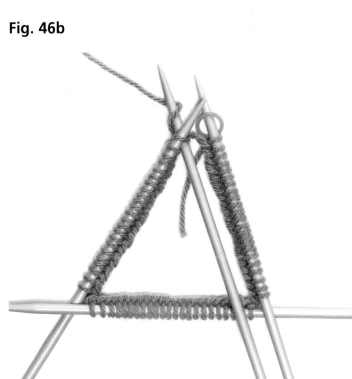

EMBELLISHMENTS

POM-POMS

Cut a piece of cardboard 3" (7.5 cm) wide and 1¼" (3 cm) long. Wind the yarn around the cardboard lengthwise until it is approximately ½" (12 mm) thick in the middle *(Fig. 47a)*.

Fig. 47a

Carefully slip the yarn off the cardboard and tightly tie an 18" (45.5 cm) length of yarn around the middle *(Fig. 47b)*. Leave yarn ends long enough to attach the pom-pom. Cut the loops on both ends and trim the pom-pom into a smooth ball *(Fig. 47c)*.

Fig. 47b

Fig. 47c

FRINGE

Cut a piece of cardboard 3" (7.5 cm) wide and ½" (12 mm) longer than you want your finished fringe to be. Wind the yarn loosely and evenly around the cardboard, then cut across one end when the card is filled; repeat as needed. Hold together half as many strands of yarn as needed for the finished fringe; fold in half. With the **wrong** side facing and using a crochet hook, draw the folded end up through a stitch and pull the loose ends through the folded end *(Fig. 48a)*; draw the knot up tightly *(Fig. 48b)*. Repeat as instructed. Lay the piece flat on a hard surface to trim the ends.

Fig. 48a

Fig. 48b

TASSEL

Cut a piece of cardboard 3" (3.75 cm) wide and as long as you want your finished tassel to be. Wind a double strand of yarn around the cardboard approximately 20 times. Cut an 18" (45.5 cm) length of yarn and insert it under all of the strands at the top of the cardboard; pull up tightly and tie securely. Leave the yarn ends long enough to attach the tassel. Cut the yarn at the opposite end of the cardboard *(Fig. 49a)* and then remove it.

Fig. 49a

Wrap another length of yarn tightly around the tassel twice, 1/2" (12 mm) below the top *(Fig. 49b)*; tie securely. Trim the ends.

Fig. 49b

FELTING BASICS

Felting is simple, just 4 easy steps. All you are really doing is shrinking and changing the texture of your knitted project!

1. START WITH WONDERFUL WOOL YARN

Read the label. AVOID "superwash" wool or wool yarns labled as machine washable as they are made, specifically, to NOT shrink. Combining novelty yarns, like ribbon or eyelash yarns, with wool yarns can give great results. Choose a novelty yarn that can be washed in hot water. For your main (felting) yarn, chose one that is at least 50% wool. Just knit the novelty yarn as a second strand along with the wool yarn. The wool will shrink and pull the novelty yarn with it. *FYI:* White and light color yarns may not felt as well as heathers or darker colors.

2. KNIT YOUR PROJECT

ALWAYS make a test swatch. Swatch with all your yarns and colors to:
- Check knit gauge.
- Make sure all the yarns in the project felt the way you want them to.
- Make sure the colors do not run.

3. MACHINE FELT

Set your top-loading washing machine for a HOT wash and COLD rinse cycle. Add about a tablespoon of detergent to the wash. Place the knitted project in a tight-mesh lingerie or sweater bag and toss into the machine. Throw in an **old** pair of jeans to speed up the felting process (the more agitation, the better). Check every 2-3 minutes during the wash cycle to keep an eye on size and shrinkage of the project. A properly felted project has shrunk to the desired size and the stitches are hard to see. When checking, you may want to wear rubber gloves to protect your hands from the hot water. Once it's felted, remove it from the machine and allow the wash water to spin out. Put the project back in for the cold rinse.

4. BLOCK (Shape and dry)

Roll the felted item in a towel and gently squeeze out the excess water. Don't wring the towel as that may set in permanent creases. Form it into the size and shape by pinning to a blocking board. Let your project air dry even though it may take several days.

PLAID DISHCLOTH

MATERIALS

100% Cotton Medium Weight Yarn
[2¹/₂ ounces, 120 yards
(70 grams, 109 meters) per ball]:
1 ball **each** Blue and White
Straight knitting needles, size 8 (5 mm)

With Blue, cast on 45 sts.

Rows 1-3: Knit across; at end of Row 3, do **not** cut Blue: 45 sts.

When instructed to slip a stitch, always slip as if to **purl (Fig. 13a, page 21)**.

Row 4: With White K4, slip 1, (K5, slip 1) across to last 4 sts, K4.

Row 5: K2, P2, slip 1, (P5, slip 1) across to last 4 sts, P2, K2; do **not** cut White.

Row 6: With Blue K7, slip 1, (K5, slip 1) across to last 7 sts, K7.

Row 7: K7, WYF slip 1 **(Fig. 13c, page 21)**, (K5, WYF slip 1) across to last 7 sts, K7; do **not** cut Blue.

Repeat Rows 4-7 until piece measures 10¹/₂" (26.5 cm) from cast on edge, ending by working Row 5. Cut White.

Last 4 Rows: With Blue, knit across.

Bind off all sts in **knit**.

STRIPED DISHCLOTH

MATERIALS

100% Cotton Medium Weight Yarn **4** MEDIUM
  [2¹/₂ ounces, 120 yards
  (70 grams, 109 meters) per ball]:
    1 ball **each** Blue and White
Straight knitting needles, size 8 (5 mm)

With Blue, cast on 44 sts.

Rows 1-4: Knit across; at end of Row 4, do **not** cut Blue.

Row 5: With White K1, [YO *(Fig. 31a, page 30)*, K2 tog *(Fig. 14, page 22)*] across to last st, K1.

Row 6: Knit across; do **not** cut White.

Rows 7-10: With Blue knit across; at end of Row 10, do **not** cut Blue.

Repeat Rows 5-10, 11 times.

Cut White.

Bind off all sts in **knit**.

Design by Eunice Svinicki.

SCARF

Finished Size: 6¼" x 45" (16 cm x 114.5 cm)

MATERIALS

Medium Weight Yarn
[1¾ ounces, 84 yards
(40 grams, 77 meters) per ball]: 3 balls
Straight knitting needles, size 10 (6 mm) **or** size
needed for gauge

GAUGE SWATCH: 4"w x 4½"h
(10 cm x 11.5 cm)
Cast on 20 sts **loosely**.
Row 1: K4, (P4, K4) twice.
Row 2: P4, (K4, P4) twice.
Rows 3-6: Repeat Rows 1 and 2 twice.
Row 7: P4, (K4, P4) twice.
Row 8: K4, (P4, K4) twice.
Rows 9-12: Repeat Rows 7 and 8 twice.
Rows 13-24: Repeat Rows 1-12.
Bind off all sts **loosely** in pattern.

SCARF
LOWER BAND

Cast on 30 sts **loosely**.

Row 1: (K1, P1) across.
Row 2: (P1, K1) across.
Rows 3-5: Repeat Rows 1 and 2 once, then
repeat Row 1 once **more**.

BODY

Row 1: P1, K1, P1, (K4, P4) 3 times, K1, P1, K1.
Row 2: K1, P1, K5, (P4, K4) twice, P5, K1, P1.
Rows 3-6: Repeat Rows 1 and 2 twice.
Row 7: P1, K1, P5, (K4, P4) twice, K5, P1, K1.
Row 8: K1, P1, K1, (P4, K4) 3 times, P1, K1, P1.
Rows 9-12: Repeat Rows 7 and 8 twice.

Repeat Rows 1-12 for pattern until Scarf
measures 44¼" (112.5 cm) from cast on edge,
ending by working Row 6 or Row 12.

UPPER BAND

Row 1: (P1, K1) across.
Row 2: (K1, P1) across.
Rows 3-5: Repeat Rows 1 and 2 once, then repeat
Row 1 once **more**.

Bind off all sts **loosely** in pattern.

BASIC MITTEN

Size	Palm Circumference	CHILDREN'S Hand Length	Thumb Length
2-4	4$\frac{1}{2}$" (11.5 cm)	3$\frac{1}{2}$" (9 cm)	1$\frac{1}{2}$" (4 cm)
6-8	5$\frac{1}{2}$" (14 cm)	4$\frac{1}{2}$" (11.5 cm)	2" (5 cm)
10-12	6$\frac{1}{2}$" (16.5 cm)	5" (12.5 cm)	2$\frac{1}{4}$" (5.75 cm)

Size	Palm Circumference	ADULTS' Hand Length	Thumb Length
Small	7" (18 cm)	6" (15 cm)	2$\frac{1}{4}$" (5.75 cm)
Medium	8" (20.5 cm)	6$\frac{1}{2}$" (16.5 cm)	2$\frac{1}{2}$" (6.5 cm)
Large	9" (23 cm)	7" (18 cm)	2$\frac{3}{4}$" (7 cm)

Size Note: Instructions are written with Children's sizes in the first set of braces { } and with Adult's sizes in the second set of braces. Instructions will be easier to read if you circle all the numbers pertaining to your size. If only one number is given, it applies to all sizes.

MATERIALS

Note: Yarn amounts are given for the total amount needed for a pair of Mittens, ranging from 160 yards (146 meters) for the two smallest sizes, 190 yards (174 meters) for the next two sizes, and 220 yards (201 meters) for the two largest sizes. When working in stripes, divide this amount between the colors used accordingly. Our Mittens are striped every two rows beginning at the Hand.

Medium Weight Yarn **MEDIUM 4**
  [3 ounces, 197 yards
  (85 grams, 180 meters) per ball]:
    {1-1-1}{1-2-2} ball(s)
Straight knitting needles, sizes 5 (3.75 mm)
  and 7 (4.5 mm) **or** sizes needed for
  gauge
Stitch holders - 2
Markers
Yarn needle

GAUGE: With larger size needles,
    in Stockinette Stitch,
    20 sts and 28 rows = 4" (10 cm)

Instructions begin on page 48.

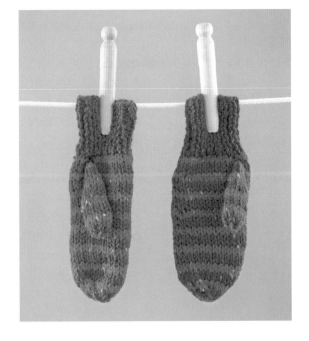

RIGHT MITTEN
CUFF

With smaller size needles, cast on
{24-28-32}{36-40-44} sts **loosely**.
Work in K1, P1 ribbing for {1½-2-2}{3-3-3}"/
{4-5-5}{7.5-7.5-7.5} cm.

HAND

Change to larger size needles.
Beginning with a **knit** row, work in Stockinette
Stitch for {2-2-4}{4-6-6} rows.

THUMB GUSSET

Row 1: K{14-16-18}{20-22-24}, place marker
(see Place Markers, page 20), right increase
(Fig. 22, page 26), K2, left increase **(Figs. 23a & b, page 26)**, place marker, knit across:
{26-30-34}{38-42-46} sts total, 4 sts between
markers.
Row 2: Purl across slipping markers.
Row 3 (Increase row): Knit to marker, slip marker,
right increase, knit to marker, left increase, slip
marker, knit across: {28-32-36}{40-44-48} sts total,
6 sts between markers.
Row 4: Purl across slipping markers.
Repeat Rows 3 and 4, {1-2-3}{4-5-6} times:
{30-36-42}{48-54-60} sts total, {8-10-12}
{14-16-18} sts between markers.

THUMB

Dividing Row: Knit to marker, slip sts just worked
onto st holder, remove marker, knit to marker,
remove marker, slip remaining sts onto second st
holder: {8-10-12}{14-16-18} sts.
Work even until Thumb measures {1-1½-2}
{2¼-2½-2¾}"/{2.5-4-5}{5.75-6.5-7} cm, ending by
working a **purl** row.
Decrease Row: K2 tog across **(Fig. 14, page 22)**: {4-5-6}{7-8-9} sts.
Cut yarn leaving a 12" (30.5 cm) end. Thread yarn
needle with end and weave through remaining sts,
pulling **firmly** to close; weave seam **(Fig. 38, page 34)**.

TOP

Row 1: With **right** side facing, slip sts from first
st holder onto right needle, slip sts from second st
holder onto left needle, with right needle, pick up
one st in Thumb seam **(Fig. 32b, page 32)**, knit
across sts on left needle: {23-27-31}{35-39-43} sts.
Row 2: Purl across.
Work in Stockinette Stitch until Mitten measures
{5-6½-7}{9-9½-10}"/{12.5-16.5-18}{23-24-25.5} cm from
cast on edge, ending by working a **purl** row.

TOP SHAPING

Row 1: K1, ★ slip 1 as if to **knit (Fig. 12, page 21)**, K1, PSSO **(Fig. 15, page 22)**,
K{6-8-10}{12-14-16}, K2 tog, K1; repeat from ★
once **more**: {19-23-27}{31-35-39} sts.
Row 2: P1, ★ P2 tog **(Fig. 17, page 24)**,
P{4-6-8}{10-12-14}, P2 tog tbl **(Fig. 19, page 24)**,
P1; repeat from ★ once **more**:
{15-19-23}{27-31-35} sts.
Row 3: K1, ★ slip 1 as if to **knit**, K1, PSSO,
K{2-4-6}{8-10-12}, K2 tog, K1; repeat from ★ once
more: {11-15-19}{23-27-31} sts.
Row 4: P1, ★ P2 tog, P{0-2-4}{6-8-10} **(see Zeros, page 20)**, P2 tog tbl, P1; repeat from ★ once **more**;
do **not** bind off: {7-11-15}{19-23-27} sts.

Size 6-8 ONLY

Row 5: K1, ★ slip 1 as if to **knit**, K1, PSSO,
K2 tog, K1; repeat from ★ once **more**; do **not**
bind off: 7 sts.

Sizes 10-12 and Adult Small ONLY

Instructions are written for size 10-12 with size
Adult Small in braces.
Row 5: K1, ★ slip 1 as if to **knit**, K1, PSSO, K2{4},
K2 tog, K1; repeat from ★ once **more**: 11{15} sts.
Row 6: P1, ★ P2 tog, P 0{2}, P2 tog tbl, P1; repeat
from ★ once **more**; do **not** bind off:
7{11} sts.

Size Adult Medium ONLY

Row 5: K1, ★ slip 1 as if to **knit**, K1, PSSO, K6,
K2 tog, K1; repeat from ★ once **more**: 19 sts.
Row 6: P1, ★ P2 tog, P4, P2 tog tbl, P1; repeat
from ★ once **more**: 15 sts.
Row 7: K1, ★ slip 1 as if to **knit**, K1, PSSO, K2,
K2 tog, K1; repeat from ★ once **more**; do **not**
bind off: 11 sts.

Size Adult Large ONLY

Row 5: K1, ★ slip 1 as if to **knit**, K1, PSSO, K8, K2 tog, K1; repeat from ★ once **more**: 23 sts.

Row 6: P1, ★ P2 tog, P6, P2 tog tbl, P1; repeat from ★ once **more**: 19 sts.

Row 7: K1, ★ slip 1 as if to **knit**, K1, PSSO, K4, K2 tog, K1; repeat from ★ once **more**: 15 sts.

Row 8: P1, ★ P2 tog, P2, P2 tog tbl, P1; repeat from ★ once **more**; do **not** bind off: 11 sts.

All Sizes

Cut yarn leaving a 20" (51 cm) end. Thread yarn needle with end and weave through remaining sts, pulling **firmly** to close; weave seam.

LEFT MITTEN

Work same as Right Mitten to Thumb Gusset.

THUMB GUSSET

Row 1: K{8-10-12}{14-16-18}, place marker, right increase, K2, left increase, place marker, knit across: {26-30-34}{38-42-46} sts total, 4 sts between markers.

Complete same as Right Mitten, beginning with Row 2 of Thumb Gusset.

Design by Marion Graham.

49

BASIC HAT

Size Note: Instructions are written with Children's sizes in the first set of braces { } and with Adults' sizes in second set of braces. Instructions will be easier to read if you circle all the numbers pertaining to your size. If only one number is given, it applies to all sizes.

MATERIALS
Note: Yarn amounts are given for the total amount needed for a Hat, ranging from 190 yards (174 meters) for the two smallest sizes, 220 yards (201 meters) for the next two sizes, and 250 yards (229 meters) for the two largest sizes. When working in stripes, divide this amount between the colors used accordingly. Our Hat is striped every two rows beginning at the Body.

Medium Weight Yarn **[MEDIUM 4]**
   [3 ounces, 197 yards (85 grams, 180 meters) per ball]: {1-1-2}{2-2-2} ball(s)
Straight knitting needles, sizes 5 (3.75 mm) **and** 7 (4.5 mm) **or** sizes needed for gauge
Markers
Yarn needle

GAUGE: With larger size needles, in Stockinette Stitch, 20 sts and 28 rows = 4" (10 cm)

RIBBING
With smaller size needles, cast on {78-84-90}{102-108-114} sts very **loosely**. Work in K1, P1 ribbing for {1-1-1}{1½-1½-1½}"/{2.5-2.5-2.5}{4-4-4} cm.

BODY
Change to larger size needles. Work in Stockinette Stitch until Body measures {3½-4-4½}{5-5½-6}"/{9-10-11.5}{12.5-14-15} cm from cast on edge, ending by working a **purl** row.

TOP SHAPING
Row 1: K{10-11-12}{14-15-16}, slip 1 as if to **knit** *(Fig. 12, page 21)*, K2 tog *(Fig. 14, page 22)*, PSSO *(Fig. 15, page 22)*, ★ place marker *(see Place Markers, page 20)*, K{10-11-12}{14-15-16}, slip 1 as if to **knit**, K2 tog, PSSO; repeat from ★ across: {66-72-78}{90-96-102} sts.

Row 2: Purl across slipping markers.

Row 3 (Decrease row)**:** Knit to within 3 sts of marker, slip 1 as if to **knit**, K2 tog, PSSO, ★ slip marker, knit to within 3 sts of marker, slip 1 as if to **knit**, K2 tog, PSSO; repeat from ★ 3 times **more**, knit across to last 3 sts, slip 1 as if to **knit**, K2 tog, PSSO: {54-60-66}{78-84-90} sts.

Row 4: Purl across slipping markers.

Repeat Rows 3 and 4, {4-4-5}{6-6-7} times; do **not** bind off: {6-12-6}{6-12-6} sts.

Cut yarn leaving a 20" (51 cm) end. Thread yarn needle with end and weave through remaining sts, pulling **firmly** to close; weave seam **(Fig. 38, page 34)**.

If desired, add pom-pom **(Figs. 47a-c, page 42)**.

Design by Marion Graham.

BOOTIES

Size: 0-3 months

MATERIALS

Super Fine Weight Yarn
[1³/₄ ounces, 286 yards
(50 grams, 262 meters) per ball]: 1 ball
Straight knitting needles, size 3 (3.25 mm) **or**
size needed for gauge
Marker
Yarn needle
¹/₄" (7 mm) wide Ribbon - 36" (91.5 cm)

GAUGE: In Stockinette Stitch,
21 sts and 27 rows = 3" (7.5 cm)

SOLE

Cast on 36 sts.
Row 1: K 17, place marker **(see Place Markers, page 20)**, knit across.
Row 2: Knit across slipping marker.
Increases are made by knitting into the front **and** into the back of the same stitch **(Figs. 20a & b, page 25)**.
Row 3 (Increase row): K1, increase, knit to within one st of marker, increase, slip marker, K2, increase, knit across to last 2 sts, increase, K1: 40 sts.
Row 4: Knit across slipping marker.
Rows 5-12: Repeat Rows 3 and 4, 4 times, removing marker on Row 12: 56 sts.

SIDES

Rows 1 and 2: Knit across.
Row 3 (Right side)**:** Purl across.
Row 4: Knit across.
Row 5: Purl across.
Rows 6 and 7: Knit across.
Row 8: Purl across.
Rows 9 and 10: Knit across.
Row 11: Purl across.
Row 12: Knit across.
Rows 13 and 14: Purl across.

INSTEP

Row 1: K 33, slip 1 as if to **knit (Fig. 12, page 21)**, K1, PSSO **(Fig. 15, page 22)**; **turn**, leave remaining 21 sts unworked.
Row 2: Slip 1 as if to **purl (Fig. 13a, page 21)**, P 10, P2 tog **(Fig. 17, page 24)**; **turn**, leave remaining sts unworked.
Row 3: Slip 1 as if to **knit**, K 10, slip 1 as if to **knit**, K1, PSSO; **turn**.
Rows 4-18: Repeat Rows 2 and 3, 7 times; then repeat Row 2 once **more**; **turn**.
Row 19: Slip 1 as if to **knit**, K 24.
Row 20: Purl across all sts: 38 sts.
Row 21 (Eyelet row)**:** [K2 tog **(Fig. 14, page 22)**, YO **(Fig. 31a, page 30)**] across to last 2 sts, K2.
Row 22: Purl across.

CUFF

Rows 1 and 2: Knit across.
Row 3: Purl across.
Row 4: Knit across.
Rows 5 and 6: Purl across.
Row 7: Knit across.
Rows 8 and 9: Purl across.
Row 10: Knit across.
Row 11: Purl across.
Rows 12 and 13: Knit across.
Row 14: Purl across.
Rows 15 and 16: Knit across.
Row 17: Purl across.
Row 18: Knit across.
Bind off all sts **loosely** in **purl**.
Sew sole and back seam. Weave an 18" (45.5 cm) length of ribbon through each Eyelet row.

Design by Barbara Johnston.

PILLOW

Finished Size: 16" (40.5 cm) square

MATERIALS

Medium Weight Yarn
[3½ ounces, 195 yards
(100 grams, 175 meters) per ball]: 2 balls
Straight knitting needles, size 7 (4.5 mm) **or** size
needed for gauge
Cable needle
Pillow form - 16" (40.5 cm) square
Fabric - ½ yard (½ meter) for lining (optional)
Yarn needle

GAUGE: In Stockinette Stitch,
20 sts and 26 rows = 4" (10 cm)

STITCH GUIDE

BACK CABLE (uses next 6 sts)
Slip next 3 sts onto cable needle and hold in
back of work *(Fig. 42b, page 37)*, K3 from left
needle, K3 from cable needle.
FRONT CABLE (uses next 6 sts)
Slip next 3 sts onto cable needle and hold in
front of work *(Fig. 42a, page 37)*, K3 from left
needle, K3 from cable needle.

BODY (Make 2)

Cast on 92 sts.
Row 1 (Right side)**:** K 16, P1, K 13, P1, K 30, P1,
K 13, P1, K 16.

Note: Loop a short piece of yarn around any stitch
to mark Row 1 as **right** side.

Row 2: P 16, K1, P 13, K1, P 30, K1, P 13, K1,
P 16.
Row 3: K 16, P1, K 13, P1, K1, K2 tog 14 times
(Fig. 14, page 22), K1, P1, K 13, P1, K 16: 78 sts.
Row 4: P 16, K1, P 13, K1, P1, (knit into the front
and into the back of the next st) 14 times *(Figs. 20a
& b, page 25)*, P1, K1, P 13, K1, P 16: 92 sts.

Row 5: K 16, P1, work Back Cable, K1, work Front
Cable, P1, K 30, P1, work Back Cable, K1, work
Front Cable, P1, K 16.
Row 6: P 16, K1, P 13, K1, P 30, K1, P 13, K1,
P 16.

Repeat Rows 3-6 for pattern until piece measures
16½" (42 cm) from cast on edge, ending by
working Row 6.

Bind off all sts in pattern.

FINISHING

Cover pillow form with fabric, if desired.

With **right** sides of Body together, sew around
3 sides; turn right side out, insert covered pillow
form and sew last side.

Design by Joyce Winfield Vanderslice.

CABLE AFGHAN

Finished Size: 45¹/₂" x 62"
(115.5 cm x 157.5 cm)

MATERIALS

Medium Weight Yarn
[3¹/₂ ounces, 195 yard
(100 grams, 175 meters) per ball]: 14 balls
31" (78.5 cm) Circular knitting needle, size 10
(6 mm) **or** size needed for gauge
Cable needle

GAUGE SWATCH: 12"w x 4"h
(30.5 cm x 10 cm)
Cast on 56 sts.
Rows 1-22: Work Rows 10-13 of Afghan, 5 times, then work Rows 10 and 11 once **more**.
Bind off all sts.

STITCH GUIDE

FRONT CABLE (uses next 4 sts)
Slip next 2 sts onto cable needle and hold in **front** of work *(Fig. 42a, page 37)*, K2 from left needle, K2 from cable needle.
BACK CABLE (uses next 4 sts)
Slip next 2 sts onto cable needle and hold in **back** of work *(Fig. 42b, page 37)*, K2 from left needle, K2 from cable needle.
TWIST (uses next 2 sts)
Working **behind** first st on left needle, knit into **back loop** *(Fig. 41, page 37)* of second st making sure **not** to drop the first stitch off, then knit the first st letting both sts drop off needle.

Cast on 182 sts.

Rows 1-7: Knit across.
Row 8: Knit across increasing 30 sts evenly spaced *(see Increasing Evenly Across the Row, page 31)*: 212 sts.
Row 9 (Right side)**:** K4, ★ P2, K2, P2, (K4, P2) twice, K2, P2, K4; repeat from ★ across.
Row 10: K6, P2, K2, (P4, K2) twice, P2, ★ K8, P2, K2, (P4, K2) twice, P2; repeat from ★ across to last 6 sts, K6.
Row 11: K4, ★ P2, work Twist, P2, (K4, P2) twice, work Twist, P2, K4; repeat from ★ across.
Row 12: K6, P2, K2, (P4, K2) twice, P2, ★ K8, P2, K2, (P4, K2) twice, P2; repeat from ★ across to last 6 sts, K6.
Row 13: K4, ★ P2, work Twist, P2, work Front Cable, P2, work Back Cable, P2, work Twist, P2, K4; repeat from ★ across.
Repeat Rows 10-13 until Afghan measures 61" (155 cm) from cast on edge, ending by working Row 11.
Next Row: Knit across decreasing 30 sts evenly spaced *(see Decreasing Evenly Across the Row, page 31)*: 182 sts.
Last 6 Rows: Knit across.

Bind off all sts in **knit**.

Design by Frances Moore-Kyle.

SCALLOP BABY AFGHAN

Finished Size: 33½" x 37½" (85 cm x 95.5 cm)

MATERIALS

Medium Weight Yarn ![MEDIUM 4]
[3½ ounces, 166 yards
(100 grams, 152 meters] per ball]: 8 balls
24" (61 cm) Circular knitting needle, size 7
(4.5 mm) **or** size needed for gauge

GAUGE: In Stockinette Stitch,
 20 sts and 26 rows = 4" (10 cm)

STITCH GUIDE

BOBBLE (uses one st)
(K, P, K) **all** in next st, **turn**, K3, **turn**, K3, slip second and third sts on right needle over first st and off needle.

Cast on 167 sts.

Rows 1-9: K1, (P1, K1) across.
Row 10 (Right side)**:** Knit across.
Row 11: Purl across.
Rows 12 and 13: Repeat Rows 10 and 11.
When instructed to slip a stitch, always slip as if to **purl (Fig. 13a, page 21)**.
Row 14: P4, WYF slip 3 **(Fig. 13c, page 21)**, (P3, WYF slip 3) across to last 4 sts, P4.
Row 15: K4, WYB slip 3, (K3, WYB slip 3) across to last 4 sts, K4.
Row 16: Knit across.
Row 17: Purl across.
Row 18: K5, ★ insert right needle under loose strands and knit together with next st **(Fig. 50)**, K5; repeat from ★ across.

Fig. 50

Row 19: Purl across.
Row 20: K5, (work Bobble, K5) across.
Row 21: Purl across.
Row 22: Knit across.
Row 23: Purl across.
Rows 24-33: Repeat Rows 14-23.
Rows 34-43: K1, (P1, K1) across.
Repeat Rows 10-43 for pattern until Afghan measures approximately 37½" (95.5 cm) from cast on edge, ending by working Row 43.

Bind off all sts in pattern.

Design by Brooke Shellflower.

DOG SWEATER

MEASURING YOUR DOG
Take neck and chest measurements **(Fig. 51)**. If measurements do **not** match a specific size **exactly**, then go to the next larger size that **does** match a measurement and follow instructions for that size.

Fig. 51

Size	Neck Measurement	Chest Measurement
Small	6½" (16.5 cm)	10½" (26.5 cm)
Medium	11½" (29 cm)	16" (40.5 cm)
Large	16" (40.5 cm)	22" (56 cm)
Ex-Large	19" (49.5 cm)	28" (71 cm)

Size Note: Instructions are written for size Small with sizes Medium, Large, and Ex-Large in braces. Instructions will be easier to read, if you circle all the numbers pertaining to your size.

MATERIALS
Medium Weight Yarn
    [3½ ounces, 195 yards
    (100 grams, 175 meters) per ball**]**:
    1{1-2-3} balls
Straight knitting needles, sizes 7 (4.5 mm) **and**
   8 (5 mm) **or** sizes needed for gauge
16{24-24-29}"/40.5{61-61-73.5} cm Circular
   needle, size 8 (5 mm)
Marker
Yarn needle
Sewing needle and elastic thread

GAUGE: With larger size needles,
   in Stockinette Stitch,
   18 sts and 24 rows = 4" (10 cm)

BACK
NECK RIBBING
With smaller size straight needles, cast on 34{56-74-88} sts **loosely**.
Work in K1, P1 ribbing for 1{1½-1½-2}"/ 2.5{4-4-5} cm.

BODY
Change to larger size straight needles.
Row 1: Knit across.
Row 2: Purl across.
Increases are made by working into the front **and** into the back of the same stitch **(Figs. 20a & b, page 25 and Fig. 24, page 27)**.
Row 3: Increase, knit across to last st, increase: 36{58-76-90} sts.
Working in Stockinette Stitch, continue to increase one st at **each** edge every row, 3{0-3-7} times **more (see Zeros, page 20)**; then increase every other row 1{6-8-10} times, ending by working a **knit** row: 44{70-98-124} sts.

UPPER LEG BAND
Row 1: P 0{3-5-8}, K 10{12-15-16}, P 24{40-58-76}, K 10{12-15-16}, P 0{3-5-8}.
Row 2 (Increase row): Increase, knit across to last st, increase: 46{72-100-126} sts.
Row 3: P1{4-6-9}, K 10{12-15-16}, P 24{40-58-76}, K 10{12-15-16}, P1{4-6-9}.
Row 4: Repeat Row 2: 48{74-102-128} sts.
Row 5: P2{5-7-10}, K 10{12-15-16}, P 24{40-58-76}, K 10{12-15-16}, P2{5-7-10}.

LEG OPENING
Row 1: K5{8-10-13}, bind off next 4{6-9-10} sts, K 29{45-63-81}, bind off next 4{6-9-10} sts, knit across: 30{46-64-82} sts in center section and 5{8-10-13} sts in **each** outer section.

All three sections of Leg Openings are worked at the same time, using separate yarn for each section.

Row 2: P2{5-7-10}, K3; with second yarn K3, P 24{40-58-76}, K3; with third yarn K3, purl across.
Row 3: Knit across; with second yarn, knit across; with third yarn, knit across.
Repeat Rows 2 and 3, 2{4-7-9} times **more**.
Closing Row: P2{5-7-10}, K3, **turn**; add on 4{6-9-10} sts **loosely (Figs. 28a & b, page 29)**, **turn**; with same yarn, K3, P 24{40-58-76}, K3, **turn**; add on 4{6-9-10} sts **loosely**, **turn**; with same yarn, K3, purl across: 48{74-102-128} sts. Cut other 2 balls of yarn.

LOWER LEG BAND

Row 1: Knit across.
Row 2: P2{5-7-10}, K 10{12-15-16}, P 24{40-58-76}, K 10{12-15-16} sts, P2{5-7-10}.
Rows 3-6: Repeat Rows 1 and 2 twice.
Continue in Stockinette Stitch until piece measures 5¹/₂{8¹/₂-11¹/₂-13}"/14{21.5-29-33} cm from cast on edge, ending by working a **purl** row.

SHAPING

Rows 1 and 2: Bind off 6{9-12-14} sts at the beginning of the next 2 rows, work across: 36{56-78-100} sts.
Row 3 (Decrease row)**:** Slip 1 as if to **knit (Fig. 12, page 21)**, K1, PSSO **(Fig. 15, page 22)**, knit across to last 2 sts, K2 tog **(Fig. 14, page 22)**: 34{54-76-98} sts.
Row 4: Purl across.
Repeat Rows 3 and 4, 5{8-11-14} times: 24{38-54-70} sts.
Work even until Sweater measures 11{17-22-25}"/28{43-56-63.5} cm from cast on edge, ending by working a **purl** row.
Leave remaining sts on needle.
Weave seam from Neck to Shaping **(Fig. 38, page 34)**.

BACK RIBBING

The total number of stitches must be an even number.
With **right** side facing and circular needle, knit across sts on needle, pick up sts evenly around Back opening **(Figs. 32a & b, page 32)**, place marker **(see Place Markers, page 20)**.
Work in K1, P1 ribbing around for 1" (2.5 cm).
Bind off all sts **loosely** in ribbing.

FINISHING

Weave elastic thread through first and last row of Neck Ribbing.

CREW NECK PULLOVER

Size	Finished Chest Measurement
32	36" (91.5 cm)
34	38" (96.5 cm)
36	40" (101.5 cm)
38	42" (106.5 cm)
40	44" (112 cm)

Size Note: Instructions are written with sizes 32 and 34 in the first set of braces { } and with sizes 36, 38, and 40 in the second set of braces. Instructions will be easier to read if you circle all the numbers pertaining to your size. If only one number is given, it applies to all sizes.

MATERIALS

Medium Weight Yarn
   [3 ounces, 197 yards
   (85 grams, 180 meters) per ball]:
      {6-6}{7-7-8} balls
Straight knitting needles, sizes 5 (3.75 mm)
   and 7 (4.5 mm) **or** sizes needed for gauge
16" (40.5 cm) Circular needle, size 5 (3.75 mm)
Stitch holders - 2
Marker
Yarn needle

GAUGE: With larger size needles,
      in Stockinette Stitch,
         20 sts and 28 rows = 4" (10 cm)

Instructions begin on page 60.

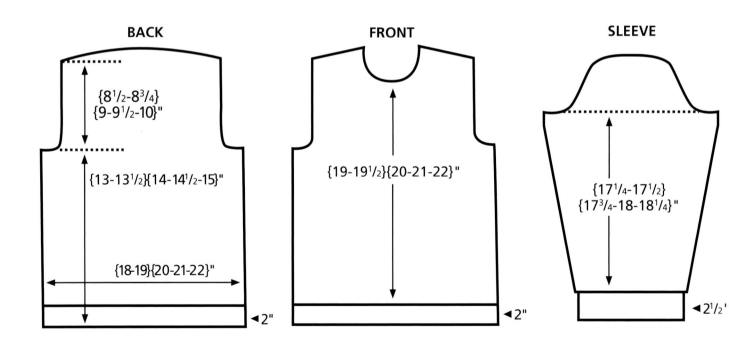

BACK   FRONT   SLEEVE

{8¹/₂-8³/₄}
{9-9¹/₂-10}"

{13-13¹/₂}{14-14¹/₂-15}"

{18-19}{20-21-22}"

{19-19¹/₂}{20-21-22}"

◄2"

◄2"

{17¹/₄-17¹/₂}
{17³/₄-18-18¹/₄}"

◄2¹/₂'

BACK
RIBBING

With smaller size straight needles, cast on {92-98}{102-108-112} sts **loosely**.

Work in K1, P1 ribbing for 2" (5 cm).

BODY

Change to larger size needles.

Work in Stockinette Stitch until Back measures {13-13½}{14-14½-15}"/{33-34.5}{35.5-37-38} cm from cast on edge **or desired length to underarm**, ending by working a **purl** row.

ARMHOLE SHAPING

Rows 1 and 2: Bind off {6-6}{6-6-8} sts at the beginning of the next 2 rows, work across: {80-86}{90-96-96} sts.
Row 3 (Decrease row)**:** K1, slip 1 as if to **knit** *(Fig. 12, page 21)*, K1, PSSO *(Fig. 15, page 22)*, knit across to last 3 sts, K2 tog *(Fig. 14, page 22)*, K1: {78-84}{88-94-94} sts.
Row 4: Purl across.
Repeat Rows 3 and 4, {6-9}{9-11-9} times: {66-66}{70-72-76} sts.
Work even until Armholes measure {8½-8¾}{9-9½-10}"/{21.5-22}{23-24-25.5} cm, ending by working a **knit** row.

SHOULDER SHAPING

Rows 1 and 2: Bind off 6 sts at the beginning of the next 2 rows, work across: {54-54}{58-60-64} sts.
Rows 3 and 4: Bind off {6-6}{6-6-7} sts at the beginning of the next 2 rows, work across: {42-42}{46-48-50} sts.
Rows 5 and 6: Bind off {6-6}{6-6-7} sts at the beginning of the next 2 rows, work across: {30-30}{34-36-36} sts.
Slip remaining sts onto st holder.

FRONT

Work same as Back until Armholes measure {6-6}{6-6½-7}"/{15-15}{15-16.5-18} cm, ending by working a **knit** row: {66-66}{70-72-76} sts.

NECK SHAPING

Both sides of Neck are worked at the same time, using separate yarn for each side.
Row 1: Purl {24-24}{24-24-26} sts, slip next {18-18}{22-24-24} sts onto st holder; with second yarn, purl across: {24-24}{24-24-26} sts **each** side.
Row 2: Knit across to within 2 sts of Neck edge, K2 tog; with second yarn, slip 1 as if to **knit**, K1, PSSO, knit across: {23-23}{23-23-25} sts **each** side.

Row 3: Purl across to within 2 sts of Neck edge, P2 tog tbl *(Fig. 19, page 24)*; with second yarn, P2 tog *(Fig. 17, page 24)*, purl across: {22-22}{22-22-24} sts **each** side.
Row 4 (Decrease row)**:** Knit across to within 2 sts of Neck edge, K2 tog; with second yarn, slip 1 as if to **knit**, K1, PSSO, knit across: {21-21}{21-21-23} sts **each** side.
Row 5: Purl across; with second yarn, purl across.
Rows 6-11: Repeat Rows 4 and 5, 3 times: {18-18}{18-18-20} sts **each** side.
Work even until Front measures same as Back to Shoulder Shaping, ending by working a **knit** row.

SHOULDER SHAPING

Rows 1 and 2: Bind off 6 sts at the beginning of the next 2 rows, work across; with second yarn, work across: {12-12}{12-12-14} sts **each** side.
Rows 3 and 4: Bind off {6-6}{6-6-7} sts at the beginning of the next 2 rows; with second yarn, work across: {6-6}{6-6-7} sts **each** side.
Row 5: Bind off {6-6}{6-6-7} sts; with second yarn, work across.
Bind off remaining sts.

SLEEVE (Make 2)
RIBBING
With smaller size straight needles, cast on {42-44}{46-46-46} sts **loosely**.
Work in K1, P1 ribbing for 2½" (6.5 cm) increasing 6 sts evenly spaced across last row **(see Increasing Evenly Across the Row, page 31 and Increases, pages 25-28)**: {48-50}{52-52-52} sts.

BODY
Change to larger size needles.
Row 1 (Right side)**:** Knit across.
Row 2: Purl across.
Rows 3 and 4: Repeat Rows 1 and 2.
Row 5 (Increase row)**:** K1, increase, knit across to last 2 sts, increase, K1: {50-52}{54-54-54} sts.
Working in Stockinette Stitch, continue to increase one stitch at each edge in same manner, every {8-8}{8-6-6} rows, {5-5}{4-1-4} times **more**; then increase every {10-10}{10-8-8} rows, {4-4}{5-10-8} times: {68-70}{72-76-78} sts.

Work even until Sleeve measures {17¼-17½} {17¾-18-18¼}"/{44-44.5}{45-45.5-46.5} cm from cast on edge, ending by working a **purl** row.

SLEEVE CAP
Rows 1 and 2: Bind off {6-6}{6-6-8} sts at the beginning of the next 2 rows, work across: {56-58}{60-64-62} sts.
Row 3 (Decrease row)**:** K1, slip 1 as if to **knit**, K1, PSSO, knit across to last 3 sts, K2 tog, K1: {54-56}{58-62-60} sts.
Row 4: Purl across.
Repeat Rows 3 and 4, {12-12}{13-14-16} times: {30-32}{32-34-28} sts.
Work even until Sleeve Cap measures {5¾-6} {6-6½-6¾}"/{14.5-15}{15-16.5-17} cm.
Bind off {3-3}{3-3-2} sts at the beginning of the next {4-2}{4-4-4} rows, work across: {18-26}{20-22-20} sts.
Bind off {4-4}{4-4-3} sts at the beginning of the next {2-4}{2-2-2} rows, work across: {10-10}{12-14-14} sts.
Bind off remaining sts.

FINISHING
Weave shoulder seams **(Figs. 34a & b, page 33)**.

NECK RIBBING
With **right** side facing and using circular needle, knit {30-30}{34-36-36} sts from Back st holder, pick up {21-22}{24-24-24} sts evenly spaced along left Neck edge **(Fig. 32b, page 32)**, knit {18-18}{22-24-24} sts from Front st holder, pick up {21-22}{24-24-24} sts evenly spaced along right Neck edge, place marker **(see Place Markers, page 20)**: {90-92}{104-108-108} sts.

Work in K1, P1 ribbing around for 1" (2.5 cm).

Bind off all sts **loosely** in ribbing.

Sew Sleeves to sweater **(Fig. 36, page 34)**.

Weave underarm and side in one continuous seam **(Fig. 38, page 34)**.

SOCKS *Shown on page 64.*

Size: Small {Medium-Large}
Finished Foot Circumference (unstretched):
6{6½-7}"/15{16.5-18} cm

Size Note: Instructions are written for size
Small with sizes Medium and Large in braces { }.
Instructions will be easier to read if you circle all the
numbers pertaining to your size. If only one number
is given, it applies to all sizes.

MATERIALS

Medium Weight Yarn **MEDIUM 4**
[3 ounces, 165 yards (85 grams, 159 meters)
per skein]: 1 skein **each** Navy, White, Tan,
Green, and Blue
Two 16" (40.5 cm) Circular knitting needles,
size 5 (3.75 cm) **or** size needed for gauge
Yarn needle
Marker

GAUGE: In ribbing (unstretched),
16 sts and 14 rnds = 2" (5 cm)

KNITTING IN THE ROUND WITH TWO CIRCULAR NEEDLES

This method is a different way for knitting
a sock than the more traditional way of the
stitches divided on three or four double pointed
needles *(Figs. 46a & b, page 41)*. Instead,
the stitches are placed on two circular needles.
Each needle is used independently of the other.
While you are knitting across the first set of the
stitches with the first needle, the second needle
will hang out of the way with its stitches at the
center of its cable. Then, you will switch to the
second needle and work across it while the first
needle hangs.

CUFF

With Tan, cast on 48{52-56} sts.

Slip the last 25{27-29} sts onto second circular
needle, placing them at the center of the cable
(Fig. 52). Push the stitches on the first needle to the
tip at the opposite end and place a marker in one
of these stitches to mark the first needle *(see Place
Markers, page 20)*.

Fig. 52

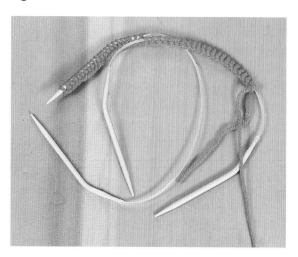

Move the first needle so that it is in front of and
parallel to the cable of the second needle *(Fig. 53)*.
Holding both needles, straighten your stitches so
that they are not twisted around the needles.

Fig. 53

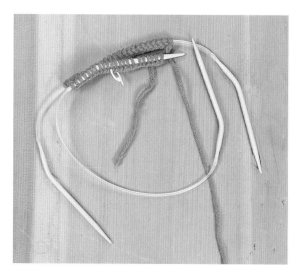

When moving from one set of stitches to the next, keep the yarn snug between the last and first stitches to prevent a hole.

Rnd 1: Using the other end of the first needle, K1, (P1, K1) across the first set of stitches.

Slide the stitches to the center of the first needle's cable and turn your work. Slide the second needle's stitches to the point of the needle and P1, (K1, P1) across.

Rnds 2-15: Work in established ribbing.
Cut Tan.
Rnds 16-27: With Blue, work in established ribbing.
Cut Blue.
With the following colors, work 6 rounds **each** in established ribbing: White, Navy, Green.
If you want a longer cuff, add more stripes to your pattern or work more rounds in each color.
Cut Green.

HEEL

With Blue, begin working in rows across stitches on first needle **only**. The stitches on the second needle will be on hold until you begin the Foot.

Row 1: P1, SSK *(Figs. 16a-c, page 23)*, P1, (K1, P1) across to last 3 sts, K2 tog *(Fig. 14, page 22)*, P1: 21{23-25} sts.
Row 2: K1, SSK, P1, (K1, P1) across to last 3 sts, K2 tog, K1: 19{21-23} sts.
Rows 3-6: Repeat Rows 1 and 2 twice: 11{13-15} sts.
Row 7: Pick up one st **purlwise** from first end of Row 5 *(Fig. 33, page 32)*, K1, (P1, K1) across, pick up one st **purlwise** from other end of Row 5: 13{15-17} sts.

Rows 8-11: Pick up one st **purlwise** from first end of next row, K1, (P1, K1) across, pick up one st **purlwise** from other end of same row: 21{23-25} sts.
Cut Blue and do **not** turn.

Instructions continued on page 64.

FOOT

Rnd 1: With Tan and second needle, pick one st **knitwise** from last rnd of Cuff **(Fig. 32b, page 32)**, P1, (K1, P1) across second needle, pick up one st **knitwise** from last last rnd of Cuff; working across first needle, P1, (K1, P1) across: 27{29-31} sts on second needle, 21{23-25} on first needle.

Rnds 2-6: Work in established ribbing. Cut Tan.

With the following colors, work 6 rounds **each** in established ribbing: White, Navy, Blue, Green, White, Tan. For largest size, work one more stripe with Blue.

TOE

Rnd 1: With Navy, work in established ribbing across second needle to last 3 sts, slip these sts onto first needle and work across: 24{26-28} sts on each needle.

Rnds 2 thru 8{9-10} (Second Needle)**:** K1, SSK, (P1, K1) across to last 3 sts, K2 tog, K1; (First Needle) SSK, (P1, K1) across to last 3 sts, K2 tog, K1: 10 sts on each needle.

Cut Navy, leaving a long end for grafting the Toe; then graft Toe **(Figs. 40a-h, pages 35 & 36)**.

Design by Peggy Schultz.

FELTED PURSE *Shown on page 66.*

Finished Size before felting:
Version A - 19"w x 16"h (48.5 cm x 40.5 cm)
Version B - 16"w x 11½"h (40.5 cm x 29 cm)
Finished Size after felting (approximate)**:**
Version A - 18"w x 11"h (45.5 cm x 28 cm)
Version B - 15"w x 10"h (38 cm x 25.5 cm)

MATERIALS *(see Felting Basics, page 43)*
VERSION A
50% Wool Super Bulky Weight Yarn **SUPER BULKY 6**
[1¾ ounces, 55 yards
(50 grams, 50 meters) per ball]:
   MC (Variegated) - 2 balls
100% Wool Medium Weight Yarn **MEDIUM 4**
[3½ ounces, 223 yards
(100 grams, 204 meters) per ball]:
   CC (Green) - 3 balls
Straight knitting needles, size 13 (9 mm) **or** size
needed for gauge

VERSION B
100% Wool Medium Weight Yarn **MEDIUM 4**
[3½ ounces, 223 yards
(100 grams, 204 meters) per ball]:
   MC (Blue) - 2 balls
   CC (Green) - 2 balls
Straight knitting needles, size 11 (8 mm) **or** size
needed for gauge

Yarn needle
Beads, jewelry, leather cord or other decorations
EXCLUSIVELY YOU PRODUCTS
13" (33 cm) double purse handles,
   Version A - Berry, item #28301
   Version B - Green, item # 28304
Brass chains, item #28341
Magnetic clasps, item #28344
Swivel clasps, item #28343

VERSION A
Work with two strands of MC and 3 strands of CC
yarn held together throughout.

VERSION B
Work with two strands of each yarn held together
throughout.

GAUGE - Version A: With MC,
in Stockinette Stitch,
12 sts and 12 rows = 4" (10 cm)

GAUGE - Version B: With MC,
in Stockinette Stitch,
15 sts and 17 rows = 4" (10 cm)

BODY
With two strands of MC, cast on 58 sts.

Row 1 (Right side)**:** Increase *(Figs. 20a & b,
page 22)*, K 12, slip 1 as if to **knit** *(Fig. 12,
page 21)*, K2 tog *(Fig. 14, page 22)*, PSSO *(Fig. 15,
page 22)*, K 12, increase twice, K 12, slip 1 as if to
knit, K2 tog, PSSO, K 12, increase.
Row 2: Purl across.
Row 3: Increase, K 12, slip 1 as if to **knit**, K2 tog,
PSSO, K 12, increase twice, K 12, slip 1 as if to **knit**,
K2 tog, PSSO, K 12, increase.
Rows 4-14: Repeat Rows 2 and 3, 4 times; then
repeat Row 2 once **more**.

Cut MC.

Row 15: With three strands of CC for Version A
and two strands of CC for Version B, repeat Row 3.
Rows 16-18: Repeat Rows 2 and 3 once, then
repeat Row 2 once **more**.

Row 19: K1, [YO *(Fig. 31a, page 30)*, K2 tog]
across to last st, K1.
Rows 20-28: Repeat Rows 2 and 3, 4 times; then
repeat Row 2 once **more**.
Row 29: K1, (YO, K2 tog) across to last st, K1.
Rows 30-34: Repeat Rows 2 and 3 twice, then
repeat Row 2 once **more**.

Cut CC.

Row 35: With two strands of MC, repeat Row 3.
Rows 36-46: Repeat Rows 2 and 3, 5 times; then
repeat Row 2 once **more**.
Bind off all sts in **knit**.

Instructions continued on page 66.

FINISHING

With **right** side facing, sew the bottom edge of the bag.

Turn **wrong** side out and sew side seam.

Felt the purse *(see Felting Basics, page 43)*.

Flip the top points of the purse down on the sides. Using yarn, sew swivels to the inside edge of the purse and clip one end of each handle to a swivel or sew one end of each handle to each side of the purse. Use the chains to wrap around the free ends of handle to join them together.

Flatten the prongs of the magnetic clasps and sew to the top inside edge of the purse with a "figure 8" stitch. Run leather cord through the eyelets formed by the yarn overs and add beads or jewelry as desired.

Design by Peggy Schultz.

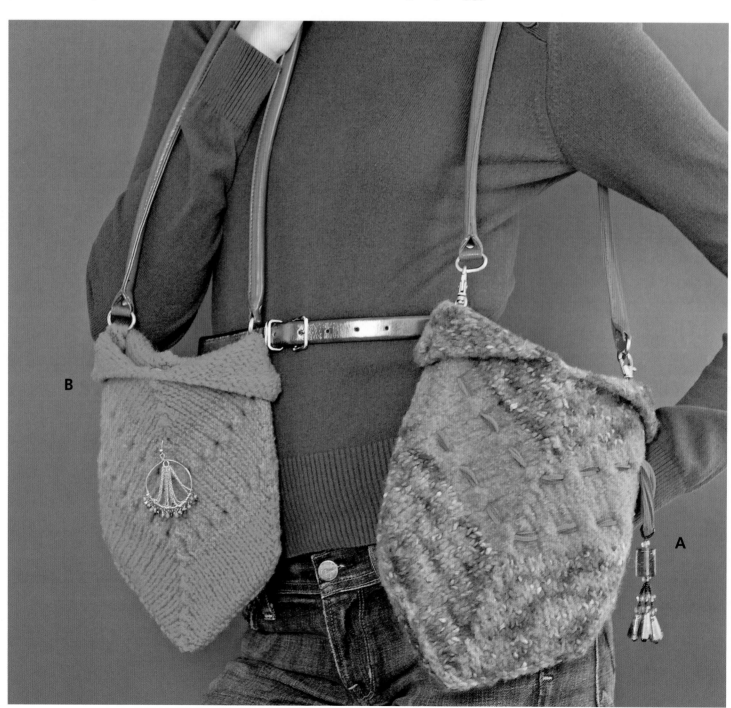

YARN INFORMATION

Projects in this leaflet were made using various weights of yarn. Any brand of specified weight of yarn may be used. It is best to refer to the yardage/meters when determining how many balls or skeins to purchase. Remember, to arrive at the finished size, it is the GAUGE/TENSION that is important, not the brand of yarn. For your convenience, listed below are the specific yarns used to create our photography models.

STRIPED DISHCLOTH
Lily® Sugar 'N Cream®
Blue - #28 Delft Blue
White - #01 White

PLAID DISHCLOTH
Lily® Sugar 'N Cream®
Blue - #28 Delft Blue
White - #01 White

SCARF
Lion® Cashmere Blend
#124 Camel

BASIC MITTEN
Lion Brand® Wool-Ease®
Solid - #112 Red Sprinkles
Striped
　　Red - #112 Red Sprinkles
　　Blue - #117 Colonial Blue

BASIC HAT
Lion Brand® Wool-Ease®
Solid - #112 Red Sprinkles
Striped
　　Red - #112 Red Sprinkles
　　Blue - #117 Colonial Blue

BOOTIES
Bernat® Baby
#00402 White

PILLOW
Bernat® Berella 4®
#8940 Natural

CABLE AFGHAN
Bernat® Berella 4®
#8940 Natural

SCALLOP BABY AFGHAN
Bernat® Satin
#04317 Star Dust

DOG SWEATER
Bernat® Berella 4®
#8929 Geranium

PULLOVER
Lion Brand® Wool-Ease®
#138 Cranberry

SOCKS
Caron® Simply Soft®
Tan - #9703 Bone
Navy - #9736 Navy
Green - #9739 Soft Green
White - #9701 White
Caron® Simply Soft® Brites
Blue - #9609 Berry Blue

FELTED PURSE
Version A
Lion Brand® Landscapes®
　　MC (Variegated) - #281 Coral Reef
Patons® Classic Wool
　　CC (Green) - #00240 Leaf Green
Version B
Patons® Classic Wool
　　MC (Blue) - #77734 Too Teal
　　CC (Green) - #00240 Leaf Green

INDEX

We have made every effort to ensure that these instructions are accurate and complete. We cannot, however, be responsible for human error, typographical mistakes, or variations in individual work.

Production Team:
Instructional Editor - Sarah J. Green
Technical Editor - Cathy Hardy
Editorial Writer - Susan McManus Johnson
Graphic Artist - Karen Allbright
Senior Graphic Artist - Chaska Richardson Lucas
Photo Stylist - Angela Alexander
Photographer - Jason Masters

Items made and instructions tested by Susan Carter, Sue Galucki, Raymelle Greening, and Kitty Jo Pietzuch.

ISBN 1-60140-099-3